Wim Wenders is a German film director, producer, photographer and writer. His internationally renowned films include *Alice in the Cities*, *Kings of the Road*, *The American Friend*, *Paris,Texas*, *Wings of Desire*, *Until the End of the World*, *Buena Vista Social Club* and many others. His groundbreaking 3D film *Pina* was nominated at the Academy Awards for Best Documentary in 2012. Wenders is president of the European Film Academy. He teaches film as a professor at the University of Fine Arts in Hamburg.

Mary Zournazi is an Australian writer and philosopher. She teaches in the sociology programme at the University of New South Wales, Sydney. She is the author of several books, including *Hope – New Philosophies for Change* and *Keywords to War: Reviving Language in an Age of Terror*.

WIM WENDERS AND MARY ZOURNAZI

INVENTING PEACE

a dialogue on perception

Hey, Joe!
Inroads to the book
that still needs
to be written!

I.B.TAURIS
LONDON · NEW YORK

20 · 3 · 2014

The two short films associated with this book can be viewed on our website: www.inventing-peace.com – the access code for *Invisible Crimes* is IBT-CRIMES, the access code for *War in Peace* is IBT-PEACE. Both films are Copyright © 2013 Wim Wenders.

All film grabs used in the book are quotations only.

Unless otherwise indicated, the photographs in this book are Copyright © 2013 Wim Wenders

Published in 2013 by I.B. Tauris & Co. Ltd
6 Salem Road, London W2 4BU
175 Fifth Avenue, New York NY 10010
www.ibtauris.com

Distributed in the United States and Canada
Exclusively by Palgrave Macmillan
175 Fifth Avenue, New York NY 10010

Copyright © 2013 Wim Wenders and Mary Zournazi

The right of Wim Wenders and Mary Zournazi to be identified as the authors of this work has been asserted by them in accordance with the Copyright, Designs and Patents Act 1988.

All rights reserved. Except for brief quotations in a review, this book, or any part thereof, may not be reproduced, stored in or introduced into a retrieval system, or transmitted, in any form or by any means, electronic, mechanical, photocopying, recording or otherwise, without the prior written permission of the publisher.

ISBN: 978 1 78076 693 5

A full CIP record for this book is available from the British Library
A full CIP record is available from the Library of Congress

Library of Congress Catalog Card Number: available

Typeset by JCS Publishing Services Ltd, www.jcs-publishing.co.uk

Printed and bound in Italy by Printer Trento

In memory of Martin Buber

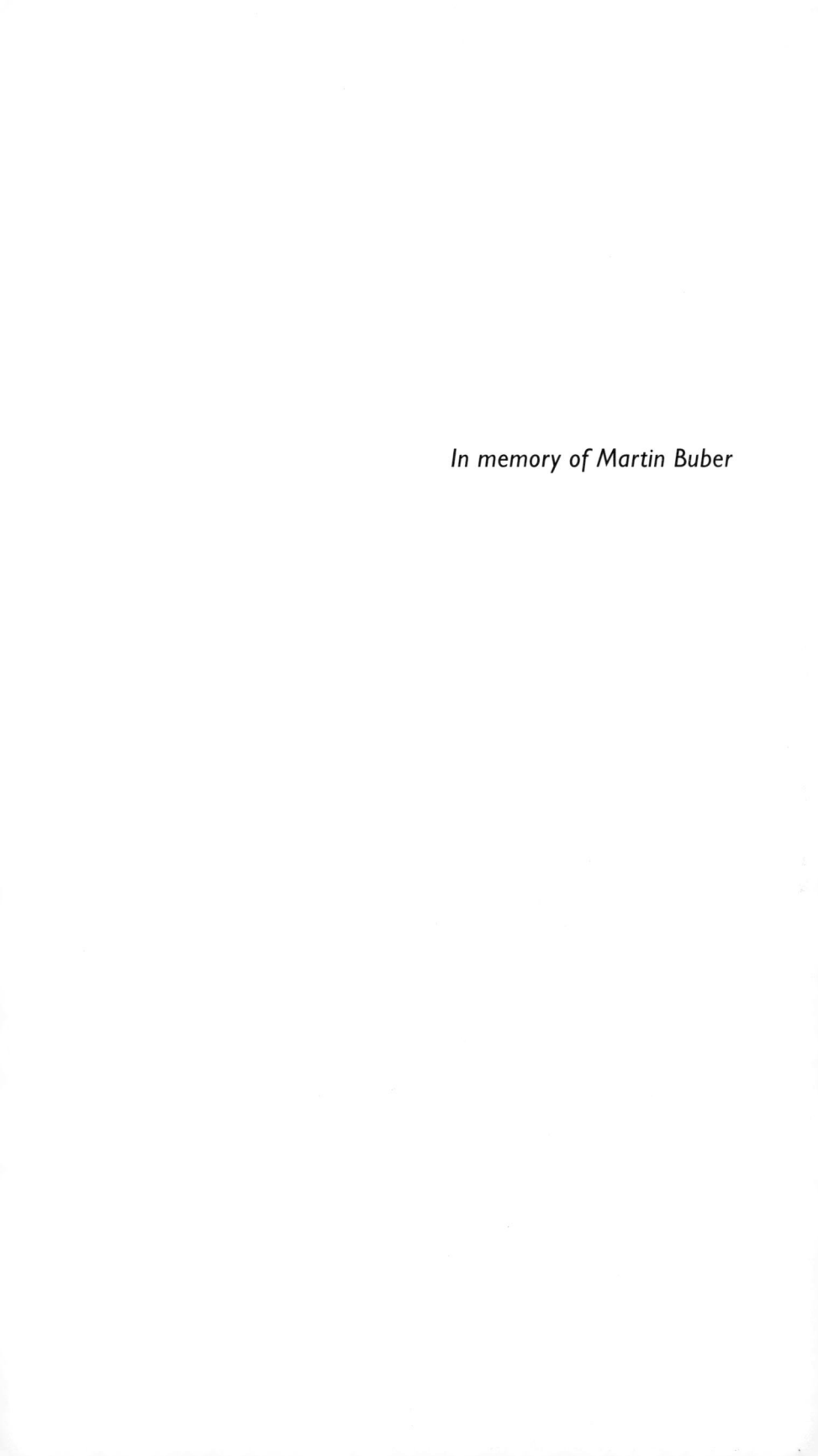

For anguish is factious: we are made to breathe easy.
                                                Gaston Bachelard

Contents

A Prelude to Looking at Peace	1
1 Meetings – Conversations on War and Peace	17
2 Inventing Peace	45
3 Enduring Images	81
4 Imagining the Real	107
5 Which Future of Seeing?	133
A Postcard from Joshua Tree	179
Postscript – Do Men Fuck it Up?!	183
Notes	196
Bibliography	204
Select Filmography	213
Acknowledgements	216

If the doors of perception were cleansed,
Everything would be appear ... as it is, infinite.
William Blake

A Prelude to Looking at Peace

Mary: Much of our everyday thinking and language is bereft of how to *imagine* and talk about peace. When I ask my friends and family how they would describe peace, the most common responses include the following: peace as the absence of war or the state of harmony in between times of conflict – something idealistic and even boring, but more often than not it is seen as unattainable. A fantasy. In many ways, this book is a response to the question, *What is peace?* and how we can imagine it; the book comes out of a specific historical context as well as a chance encounter.

I begin with a story of how Wim Wenders and I met, how we came to start this book and how we considered this question of peace.

encounters

On the eve of the second Gulf War in 2003 much of the world divided itself along the lines of good versus evil, war versus peace. The repercussions of 9/11 were still felt as the sequence of events unfolded and public dialogue and any hopeful diplomacy had evaporated. At that time, I had finished a book on hope; the book posed a series of questions and considered hope in everyday life and politics, but as events started to unfold, the question of peace arose with urgency.[1] A moral sensibility and vocabulary of what peace might mean were absent from the public debate just as much as they have been largely absent from history.

During this time, I had been invited to give a public talk at a Sydney event. The audience were hostile to my reflections on hope, my questioning of the looming war. I felt like a sacrificial lamb to slaughter, the violence contained in the audience was directed toward me, much like the sacrificial violence that humans can so readily manufacture in times of war.

Many in the Sydney audience felt I was deluded in talking about ideas of hope and peace in such circumstances of perceived evil and threat; the event was sobering. It made me realise how much we structure public debate and argument like battlefields, since my argument was so readily conquered and annihilated without any space for genuine dialogue. It seemed to me that for *real* events to touch us deeply they must resonate for us in direct and meaningful ways.[2] The language and sensibility of peace had yet to be invented.

Everything seemed bleak at that time, but my thoughts turned to a new project: peace. I didn't know what peace might mean but I knew it was necessary. I was looking for some way to kick-start the project, and it came: the German film director Wim Wenders was visiting Sydney to give some talks and in preparation for his photographic exhibition *Pictures from the Surface of the Earth*. He was a guest on a national radio programme, and by chance I had turned on the radio and I heard the last part of his hour-long interview; among other things, he reflected on his interest in peace.

Wim's radio presence was a gift. This spurred our first encounter and meeting, our first dialogues; the project was born out of this moment in time and from our mutual interest in peace.

connexions[3]

Around this time, I accompanied my mother through a long and terminal illness. I stopped thinking about peace at a global level, but became immersed in it in a very everyday way – that is, the holy and the sacred became real to me. I can only describe it as a time of reckoning for me; the sacred sits very much in the question of peace that I had yet to understand.

It was late spring when my mother died. At the time of her death and immediately afterwards, when I was alone with her for the first time, I felt her presence. The light and energy of the room had been transformed. Sitting next to her, I felt such serenity in the wake of the death and its calamity, I felt the presence of the holy: it was everyday and real. It provided a kind of solace and connexion I hadn't experienced before. The word 'holy' shares its etymological root with 'wholeness'. There was a sense of the wholeness at this time, a strange kind of unity of time and space; I felt the power and mystery of *this* world that joins us to the infinite, a sacredness that is pre-eminently real.

The German philosopher Rudolf Otto suggests that this 'power' or the idea of the holy has an awesome quality that exists alongside our usual understanding of the sacred as tied to morality or the good. The sacred has awesome qualities that are terrifying and beautiful; my mother's death was awesome and shocking to me, but it demanded respect and reverence. I felt the devastation and beauty that only such moments can bring. And it is

a prelude to looking at peace

in such moments that understandings of compassion, beauty and grace are enhanced as well as how we might understand this ethical life.

Just before her death, my mother recounted a story: she had been dozing on her bed in the early afternoon, resting after a difficult night's sleep, she was in a lot of pain. In this semi-conscious state she felt a tap on her shoulder; at first she thought it was my father, who was outside mowing the grass, but she could hear the running motor of the lawnmower and after a moment she realised it was not him. She told me 'they' had come for her. My mother was a deeply religious woman. I knew what she meant. It was her calling. The angels had come. She was ready. Two weeks later she died.

Over the years, this strange calling of angels, the sacred and peace, resonated with me through Rainer Maria Rilke's poetry just as it did for Wim in the making of his 1987 film *Wings of Desire*. It is this kind of sacred power and mysterious quality of peace that provide our connexion and yearnings for it. The opening sequence of Rilke's *Duino Elegies* declares:

> Who, if I cried, would hear among the Angels'
> Orders? and even if one of them pressed me
> suddenly to his heart: I'd be consumed
> in his potent being. For beauty is nothing
> but the beginning of terror, which we can still barely endure,
> and while we stand in wonder it coolly disdains
> to destroy us. Every Angel is terrifying.

> *Wer, wenn ich schriee, hörte mich denn aus der Engel*
> *Ordnungen? und gesetzt selbst, es nähme*
> *einer mich plötzlich ans Herz: ich verginge von seinem*
> *stärkeren Dasein. Denn das Schöne ist nichts*
> *als des Schrecklichen Anfang, den wir noch grade ertragen,*
> *und wir bewundern es so, weil es gelassen verschmäht,*
> *uns zu zerstören. Ein jeder Engel ist schrecklich.*[4]

Much like a prayer, Rilke's elegies resonate with the memory of the eternal as well as marking the sacred as pre-eminently real; that is, the poetry gives us a feel for both mystical encounters and first-hand experience. This experience might be the difference between 'to know' and 'to understand'. As Otto suggests, the mysterious quality of the sacred is by no means tantamount to 'unknowableness'; however, we might say that *knowing* peace in this regard has yet to 'passeth understanding'.[5]

*

time and the sacred

To talk about the sacred today is to consider the time and space in which value and meaning take shape; we are aware of the paradoxes that can emerge from such a statement. For instance, we are not writing about the holy and 'holy wars'; rather we are considering how the sacred is the bridge between the worlds of violence and the worlds of peace. There is a difference between theological imperialism and the sacred as a reckoning that challenges our cultural habits. This reckoning evolves through stories, images and perceptions that can encourage different ways of seeing the world and different ways of understanding peace.

Quintessentially, peace is the imagining of a different world, but a world that already surrounds us – it is the making and unmaking of ritual and tradition in our everyday lives inasmuch as it is holy and sacred. It involves 'becoming aware' as the philosopher Martin Buber would put it. This becoming aware is a special kind of observation or of looking at the world that involves compassion, grace and care. The everyday and the holy involve a care *toward* the future, this care involves an ethics that is founded in the relations between the infinite and the everyday.

English-born author Aldous Huxley suggests that revolutionary talk or philosophy identifying the world or the 'spiritual' as solely future oriented cannot provide the conditions for liberty and peace. Huxley writes,

> The peace that passes all understanding is the fruit of liberation into eternity; but in its ordinary everyday form peace is also the root of liberation. For where there are violent passions and compelling distractions, this ultimate good can never be realized. That is one of the reasons why the policy of correlated eternity-philosophies is tolerant and non-violent. The other reason is that the eternity, whose realization is the ultimate good, is a kingdom of heaven within. Thou art That; and though That is immortal and impassible, the killing and torturing of individual 'thous' is a matter of cosmic significance, inasmuch as it interferes with the normal and natural relationship between individual souls and the divine eternal Ground of all being. Every violence is, over and above everything else, a sacrilegious rebellion against the divine order.[6]

techniques for peace

From our encounters and investigations into peace it seems that much of the hindrance to peace revolves around the question of *how we look at the world but do not see it* when there is so much violence, injustice and suffering. Ours is the century of the image as never before. There are so many images circulating the globe with ever increasing speed that we *look* at all the time, but we do not have the means or the skills any more to see. What are the ethical and moral consequences of looking but not seeing? We consider this question as one of the fundamental questions of our times.

French philosopher Maurice Merleau-Ponty once noted that the subject of perception is the subject of power; in other words, how we see is what prescribes the ethical and power relations that constitute our everyday and social worlds. More precisely, he writes,

> [...] the problems of knowing what is the subject of the State, of war, etc are exactly of the same type of problem of knowing what is the subject of perception: one will not clear up the philosophy of history except by working out the problem of perception.[7]

As Italian filmmaker Michelangelo Antonioni wrote, *seeing* is the necessity of a filmmaker, seeing is central to the art of filmmaking.[8] We can say cinema makes us aware of the perception of time; each film is made of different moments that all together transform the space and time of seeing. In this way, cinema opens the potential for a modern ethics as it relates to how we see and how we make sense of the world – cinema conveys uncanny fiction as well as a kind of truth. It was our mutual interest in ways of seeing and in cinema as a space for modern ethics that brought Wim and me together to explore the problems of perception today. To investigate the questions of time, space and being, the ethical implications and the conditions for peace, we need to consider that ethical peace is distinct from political peace as such.

Throughout our book, we explore how to change our habitual ways of seeing that alienate us from each other and our sense of belonging. 'Seeing' here involves all of our senses, memory and technologies, since to look today is a combination of all these factors: the methods or techniques in which we constitute our self, our ethical realm and our encounters with each other. We consider the difference between 'seeing' and 'showing' in a technological world; how to bring together the world of technology, the sacred and *the future of seeing*.

As sociologist Émile Durkheim has written, the sacred emerges out of the techniques and rituals that are created by us. The sacred is a social reality. At a fundamental level, the images, rites and rituals that we create provide the conditions for peace in a worldly sense, how we might live and inhabit this world, and how we might imagine it. As Durkheim puts it,

> The ideal society is not outside the real society; it is part of it. Far from being torn between them, as between two mutually repellent poles, we cannot insist on one without insisting on the other. For a society is not simply constituted by the mass of individuals who compose it, by the land they occupy, by the things they use, by the movements they make, but above all by the idea that it fashions of itself.[9]

conversations

That our first conversations were initially born out of new technologies – through the internet and email exchanges – makes us think of a new generation of messengers and angels. French philosopher Michel Serres' book *Angels: A Modern Myth* looks at the possibilities of technology and new communication networks today.[10] Serres explains the necessity of considering angels and their images throughout history as just as relevant in today's technological worlds and messages. He writes that today message-bearers are brought about by the science of new technologies and universal communications – worldwide networks and cities, ceaseless activities that are mapping a new world of planetary problems. Alongside these universal message-bearing systems new forms of unspeakable injustices, poverty, wars and inequality have arisen. Serres asks:

> Are these the signs of a new legend of angels, these interchanges and annunciations, networks and visitations, demons fallen from grace, powers and dominions – are they all part of the search for mercy and redemption?[11]

We consider the question of angels, the new annunciations of images and the grace and mercy that can inspire peace, in the conversations and letters and throughout the book.[12]

Peace contains what is chaotic as well as all that is enduring. Peace is not conflict resolution per se; it is a method or technique that emerges out of the world when it is lived more truthfully, more honestly, with care, compassion and trust just as it involves active curiosity. As Serres writes,

We must decide on peace among ourselves to protect the world, and peace with the world to protect ourselves.[13]

Or, to put it another way, we must invent peace.

*

Wim: Of course it wasn't up to Mary and me to
come up with a new concept of peace.
But the necessity for its reinvention was a big realisation for us,
the very starting point for our collaboration.
The challenge for this book was obvious:
how to even reflect about peace, from scratch?
How to offer it to creative imagination again?

I had never given the notion of peace much thought. I
just always took it for granted
that there was a common understanding of what peace was. We
probably all assume that it is such an obvious idea, shared by all
of humankind,
that we didn't notice how it evaporated in
front of our eyes.

I remember I always got angry every time
when President Bush used the word 'peace' in his speeches.
The word 'freedom' as well,
backed by those politics, meant its sheer opposite.
Politicians have that way of making not only words meaningless, but
language as such.
They have a way to make words so devoid of their original significance
that they become empty shells that actively hide
how and why they can possibly concern us. You'd
really need a child to pronounce 'peace' or a poet to
use it,
but poets have given up using such big words,
– and they really don't have any other choice –
and for children it is too obvious a need to name it.
Sometimes to hear 'peace' pop up in a song,
or to see it spray-painted on a wall,
makes it echo somewhere deep in our bodies.

Mary and I tried to look for the traces of those echoes. In conversations at first,
face to face as well as in e-mails,
and then we started sending each other bits of texts.
A sort of 'dia-flow' emerged from our different practices,
which then started to shape and structure this book.
Mary and I certainly have our very own ways to write and imagine things,
but we felt this very diversity was useful for our purpose.
We hope that the reader can cope
with both of our idiosyncrasies and styles.

I'm not a philosopher,
not even an intellectual,
and I'm certainly not trying to sound like either.
My writing style (which you see here for the first time in our book)
does not pretend to look like poetry,
or even try to evoke, let alone imitate it.
It is simply my reflexive style of writing.
It helps me structure my thoughts,
and as I am rather a filmmaker and photographer,
therefore some sort of 'thinker in imagery',
writing like this helps me 'see my thoughts'.
I can think much better while I am typing
than while I am talking.
And as my handwriting is such
that I have to make an effort of deciphering it the next day,
the computer has doubled my creative possibilities or efforts.
I can immediately look at my chain of thoughts.
(Mary calls it a 'train of thought',
and she is probably right there,
but somehow I do see it more as a chain than a train,
so, for once, I leave that expression uncorrected here.)

Mary, with her background, is much more of a writer and philosopher,
definitely more trained as a scholar than me.
When we tossed ideas back and forth,
she knew where they had appeared before,
or who had actually *thought* them
– and most of the time expressed them so much clearer than us.
And so, in this book, it became mostly her part
to quote from all the wealth of thinking
in that territory of peace that we ventured into

a prelude to looking at peace

(and we do refer to many philosophers, painters, poets,
photographers and filmmakers along the way
to do justice to the subject we are raising).
I'm more of an intuitive mind than an academic one.
I follow a thought as if nobody had ever thought it before.
That's my only path into the realm of ideas.
I noticed that, when I tried to study philosophy
(which I did before I became a filmmaker).
I easily got lost entering the realm of great thinkers.
With great effort I could follow, yes,
but the very fact that it was a predetermined process
bothered me enormously.
I understood, but the understanding was fragile and unsubstantial.

Nothing stayed with me in the long run, especially if I only read it.
Briefly, I did not gain knowledge this way,
nothing affected me existentially,
whereas anything I could see and shape on my own
became a lasting form of 'mental possession'
and would actually 'concern' me.
So I always figured that 'learning' was much more successful,
if I did it on my own.
Make my own mistakes, shape my own insight and recognition.

I thereby soon recognised, and gladly so,
that my ambition could never be to create anything 'new'.
Doing things my way from scratch
did not necessarily produce unseen, unthought-of
or unheard-of ideas and images.
'Originality' is an illusion, most of the time,
whatever field we're working in,
and usually overrated.
Not many of us are born geniuses.
Finding our own approach, however,
discovering in ourselves ideas or recognition born from curiosity,
honesty or conviction,
that is something every man and woman can claim,
all on their own,
no matter how many people have the same convictions,
have come to the same conclusion
or believe in the same things as true.

That's why you'll find in our book many a detour, many a clumsy effort,
many contradictions, repetitions or new thought launches.
We don't have an answer for the peace question.
We just looked at it from many sides,
hoping that some of our approaches
might tempt you to try and follow them,
offer you new angles and associations
or give you reasons to disapprove.
Anything, at this point, we felt,
that fills the word with some new taste,
that makes it reappear in front of your inner eye,
or that gives you a longing for wanting it to reverberate somehow,
in your imagination, in your everyday life,
anything was helpful to reanimate the 'peace process' in our minds.
Our book is neither based entirely on theory nor on practice.
We rather used both, from our different perspectives and experiences,
to stir our thoughts (and maybe yours) in different directions,
so that our own (and we hope your)
habitual ways of reflecting about peace
were brought to reorient or refocus.

Our book is an invitation to think along,
to enter our dialogue and make it a flow and exchange of ideas,
to look at the perception of peace
and to contemplate what it can mean to you
(and maybe to you and us only).
Thinking *together* made us realise
how much of 'the peace process' only emerges out of a common effort.

Mary being from Australia and me from Germany
seemed to be a symbolic gesture for such an invitation, we felt.
We come from different parts of the world,
almost from antipodes, at least geologically speaking.
She travelled to Berlin for some of our encounters,
I travelled to Australia on several occasions,
and we met in different 'in-between' places,
in Los Angeles, Montréal, Tokyo, Toronto and Joshua Tree.
And then we were a woman and a man,
not to overstate that fact.
We all know how gender is always a mixture of conditions,
not just a single propensity.
But I feel very strongly

a prelude to looking at peace

that any actual 'peace process' on this planet,
political, sociological, ethical,
needs to involve women in a big way.
It bothers me deeply to see any congregation of politicians
and start counting the few (if any) women in the pack.
It bothers me even more when I look at Israel and Palestine.
Sometimes I just want to shout:
'Give all these men a rest and let the women step in!'
That alone might not be a solution,
but male 'pragmatics' have proved for too long to
be the wrong approach to peace,
or even worse: to have blocked access to it.

Unblocking that access is the hope for this book.

*

Mary: For us, inventing peace is making peace visible in a new way. We reflect on various film, literary, philosophical and artistic examples that historically precede us to engage with questions that haunt us more forcibly today. In this approach, we look closely at creative works that demonstrate an approach to peace through sacred, ethical and spiritual means, to provide an alternative to the inhumanity of war and violence. Our choices constitute how we imagine peace: the slow and careful consideration of images, a genuine dialogue and meeting of different ideas and perspectives.

For our process of writing together we are indebted to Martin Buber's understanding of dialogue as 'genuine meeting' or encounter with others. We are also grateful to quantum physicist David Bohm's idea of dialogue as the artful process and flow between people that offers the potential for change. For Bohm, every moment contains a flow of meaning or movement, the co-presence of different realities; language itself is a social presence of this flow of meaning, the implicate order of things. He writes, 'Meaning enfolds the whole world into me, and vice-versa – that enfolded meaning is unfolded as action, through my body and then through the world.'[14] For Bohm, twenty-four frames per second of the moving image gives a visual picture of this flow – how we see at any given moment in time – as well as the connection to the continuous flow and movement of a universal order, the unity and connection of histories, actions and ideas. In these moments of flow, meaning can take shape and the co-presence of languages and actions, histories and ideas, come together in artful ways, in the creation of something new, in our case, this *dia-flow* of writing.

For Buber, genuine dialogue is the fundamental relationship and gateway in this life as well as the holy. This dialogue is not limited to humans but includes all that we encounter in this world; it is in our genuine meetings and encounters in this world that real value and relationships can be developed and exchanged. And it is in these dialogues that we encounter what Buber might call a 'four-dimensional reality'. The silent words on the page inhabit this flow of meaning, this four-dimensional reality in this space between I-and-you.

Inventing peace involves a genuine dialogue with the world and ourselves so that we can transform our habitual ways of looking at it. Economic, legal and political actions to prevent war and to protect human rights are fundamental to any quest for peace, yet at the same time, if we do not invent new ways of looking at these questions, we remain locked in habitual political patterns of power and resistance.

Without a certain spiritual dimension of grace, humility and care, the quest for peace may not embrace a real sense of justice for others and ourselves. From this perspective, peace – rather than being a static idea – is a *continual* process of transformation and change. Our book hopes to offer some techniques (or *teckne* in the Greek sense of the word: arts, skills or crafts) for peace that can enable us to better *see* and remind us of the world's soulfulness, uniqueness and beauty; that is, to be re-enchanted with the world once again, and to create the conditions for peace. Rilke writes:

> For gazing, you see, sets limits.
> And the more truly gazed-at world
> wants to grow boundless love.

> Work of the eyes is done,
> begin heart-work now
> on those images in you, those captive ones;
> for you overpowered them: but you don't yet know them.
> Behold, inner man, your inner woman,
> she who was won
> from a thousand natures, she
> the till now *only* won

> *Denn des Anschauns, siehe, ist eine Grenze.*
> *Und die geschautere Welt*
> *will in der Liebe gedeihn.*

> *Werk des Gesichts ist getan,*
> *tue nun Herz-Werk*

*an den Bildern in dir, jenen gefangenen; denn du
überwältigtest sie: aber nun kennst du sie nicht.
Siehe, innerer Mann, dein inneres Mädchen,
dieses errungene aus
tausend Naturen, dieses
erst nur errungene, nie
noch geliebte Geschöpf.*[15]

Handshake Peter Falk and Damiel (Bruno Ganz)
(from *Wings of Desire*, 1987)

All real living is meeting.

Martin Buber

Meetings – Conversations on War and Peace

Mary: This chapter is a record and chronology of our initial conversations, 'mailversations' and thoughts on peace, as our response to a time of war. It is also tracking some of our mutual considerations toward our common book project.

It all began with a conversation between the two of us in November 2003. I spoke of my mother's death, and her story of angels that brought the appearance of the sacred in the everyday closer to me. Wim had just opened an exhibition on angels in movies at the Berlin Film Museum; he sent me his opening address, and so angels became the starting point for our dialogues on peace. Our initial correspondence took place over Christmas and New Year 2003–4 and responded very much to the second Gulf War crisis. These dialogues continued until July 2006 by email letters and correspondence.

*

opening the Angel exhibition at the Berlin Film Museum

'An angel crosses the room',
we say, when several people are gathered, talking,
and there is a sudden silence.
But why?

Is it some sort of awe that is expressed in this saying?
Don't we also feel uncomfortable,
because the sudden silence is awkward,
and everybody is just waiting for somebody
to come up with something to say to break the silence?

The angel crosses the room,
and all of a sudden we feel his (or her) presence.
How real is it?
What if we could actually SEE him, or her?

Encounters with angels are always described
as starting with quite a shock.
The eruption of the transcendental into our life,
of the supernatural or the Metaphysical,
is first witnessed with a great deal of anxiety.
Understandably so:
these are indeed creatures from a different world.

'Don't be afraid!' is the angel's first line, inevitably.
That's their main concern, the ethics of their profession, so to speak,
to achieve the opposite of fear.
They want to evoke JOY, SECURITY, BLESSING,
the very absence of fear.

Their diabolic counterparts
have been much more successful in movies,
those demons, vampires, monsters, witches
and other horror creatures.
The appearances of 'good spirits' in movies
are more sporadic, that's for sure.
Probably because they represent a bigger challenge.

Piece of cake, to spread fear,
but the opposite, to personify LOVE,
that's a tough one.
If you want, angels are so much better people
than we could ever manage to be,
especially in the field of love.

Where we are selfish, only too often, they are self-less,
where we turn jealous, they remain cool, calm and collected.
Any of our defaults, and all our vices, are unknown to them.

Their loving look upon us ...
you could read that as a metaphor for cinema.

> A film camera and film crews can do everything angels can do.
> Remain invisible.
> Cross walls (even THE wall, at the time),
> watch us from way above or listen to our most secret dreams.
>
> Cinema in its most precious moments
> and in the great works of film history
> is indeed HEAVEN ON EARTH.

December 2003/January 2004

Mary: I've been thinking that angels and fear are our starting points to talk about peace. Beginning there, since peace is very much about angels – at least that is my feeling – there is something in the awesome qualities of angels that connects us with peace ...

Wim: Amazingly enough, angels are often depicted as 'warriors', carrying mighty swords and armour. One would rather assume that they are messengers of peace, and therefore not in need of any weaponry. But apparently that's not the case. And their first line inevitably is: 'Don't be afraid!' So they must be scary, or at least awe-inspiring, at first sight. Which makes me wonder if, according to the angels, peace could in fact be something that needs to be fought for, or that needs to be protected with weapons, somehow ...

Now that sounds suspiciously close to the way of thinking which led the present American administration to a pre-emptive war, and not unlike the principles which have determined Israeli politics towards Palestine for decades now. So maybe the angels didn't get things right? Maybe they need to be disarmed?

I'm exaggerating. The angels are not at fault. It is their DEPICTION that is certainly flawed by our human thinking, or, rather, that is determined by the wishful thinking of the human race. Images of angels say more about the state of mind of their painters and describe their worldly cultures better than the spiritual realm of the angels themselves. Men, in their entire history, have preferred the careers of warriors to those of peace-seekers. We'd have to disarm our genes first, thousands of years of battles fought, in order to imagine the peace that must govern an angel's mind. And THAT'S why they first say: 'Don't be afraid!' They just know our convoluted thinking. They know that nothing scares us more than the unknown.

That's why I come to think that 'absence of fear' must be the most fundamental definition of peace. Only where there is no fear, is there no need to defend. And only if there is no readiness for defence, is there also no willingness to attack. There is an old air-raid shelter near the Anhalter Bahnhof, in Berlin, some leftover from World War Two. (You can see it in *Wings of Desire* in the background of the scene in which the ex-angel Peter Falk offers a hand-shake to Damiel, the angel played by Bruno Ganz.) In the Fifties and Sixties, they tried to get rid of these monster concrete blocks in the middle of the city, but didn't succeed in destroying them, even with massive amounts of dynamite. So they still stand there, unused, unusable, monuments to the horrors of war that started in Berlin and that eventually destroyed the city itself. On the side of this particular 'Bunker', somebody had painted in big letters: 'Wer Bunker baut, baut auch Bomben' (Those who build bomb shelters, build bombs, too). That is the essence of it. You can't separate attack from defence, and President Bush just brought this to its ugliest conclusion with the first pre-emptive war in American history. (I leave it to the historians to state who were the other politicians of the twentieth century who did so. You can guess twice.) Sadly, it seems that our human genes back up George W. Bush. To hit first, so you can't be hit, is a strategy that has worked since Neanderthal man. It isn't exactly biblical. Christianity really suggests the opposite. But even Bush's own interpretation of religion seems to back him up. All he needed to do was turn time back a little bit. The medieval thinking of Islamic fundamentalism is quite compatible with medieval Christianity.

If FEAR is the primary issue and the core of aggression – therefore the biggest stumbling block for PEACE – it is necessary to define 'fear'. I suggest: 'absence of faith'. Again, that's why the angels start their encounters with humans saying: 'Don't be afraid!' They could just as well say: 'Have faith!' Somebody with faith would not or could not be afraid. Now that does not limit 'faith' to 'religious belief' at all. You could just as well define 'faith' as 'equipped with a solid structure of security', or 'rooted in an unshakable identity'.

In a way, the angels suggest to the men and women they meet that they should step up to their level of confidence. 'Come enter the kingdom of trust, where fear is unknown.' They want to meet humankind on that platform. Of course, we call that 'Heaven', but we could just as well call such a world without fear more prosaically 'Civilisation'. Why haven't we reached that state yet, why did humanity lapse so badly after the end of the Cold War? Remember our hopes when the Berlin Wall fell? Didn't we all think that this was the true threshold for the twenty-first century, the dawn of the age of civilisation, where wars would finally cease? Well, we can only state that we missed that mark badly. The world is more deeply rooted in fear than before; 'absence of fear' appears more utopian than ever, since 9/11. Is that only the fault of fanatic Muslim fundamentalism?

Consider 'absence of fear' as a two-fold thing. It both demands to not HAVE fear, and to not INDUCE it. Fundamentalist-driven terrorism, as we have experienced it for a few years now, tries to pull us all down into its medieval pit. Once we have allowed them to drag us down there and to meet them on THEIR territory, we have lost the battle already. They have won by just making us agree to their rule: FEAR. The willingness to have fear implies the willingness to pass it on.

American politics should have never declared 'WAR' on terrorism. That both upgraded terrorists to soldiers (which they already were in their own imagination, but now the world confirmed that twisted belief...) and brought our own morals down to theirs: into the pits. Just see what Bush did to the Bill of Rights. Just picture Guantánamo. Just take all the lies that have been spread for the last two years in order to maintain that self-fulfilling prophecy of 'War on Terrorism'. The entire war on Iraq was such a concoction of lies. These politics were necessarily doomed, from the beginning, to produce and to accumulate more fear (apart from making some profit along the way). They certainly do not qualify to enter the platform of Twenty-First-Century Civilised Life.

There WAS an alternative, but, unfortunately, too many people have forgotten that it existed. For a small loophole in time, in late September and early October 2001, as America was mourning, and as it had ALL the world's sympathy, there was that potential of hope and of a future for peace. The remote possibility of another way of thinking. The vague realisation that the 'Right of the Stronger' could be replaced by the 'Right of the Wiser'. But then the opposite happened and Bush imposed the 'Right of the Foolish', combining American Strength with a desire for Revenge, and coupled with an unhealthy greed for influence, resources and profit. Anyway, in that loophole in time, an alternative existed (now utopian, but not then ...), and that would have been the 'War on Injustice'. Not to fight the symptoms of terrorism, but rather their roots: Poverty and Inequality. Too late now to speculate about it, how that would have decapitated Terrorism, instead of pushing millions towards it... Hey, maybe it wasn't even such a foolish utopian alternative. I remember that I even heard the president of the World Bank state something on CNN to the effect that terrorism could only be fought at the root, which was inequality and the widening gap between the rich and the poor, the informed and the uninformed.

Mary: You have said angels evoke joy, security, blessing as opposed to fear. The great challenge, then, is to find ways to demonstrate the exuberance of joy and possibility. So it's not just 'absence of fear' necessarily but making visible the other qualities of living that exist and surround us ...

Wim: Exactly. Good to keep in mind what other feelings can replace fear, if you dare to support them. 'Joy', 'Trust', 'Security', 'Blessing' – all those synonyms for 'Peace' which the angels evoke and of which they are messengers. But their counterparts are not only more successful in movies, they are more successful in communication in general. The other, more real, 'axis of evil', so to speak, rejoices in an exuberance of dread and fright and panic, in the news as well as in movies. To watch the remake (!) of *Texas Chainsaw Massacre* in early 2004 and to read jubilant and glorifying reviews of it, and to see the original (in hindsight) brought into the context of a piece of art that helped Americans cope with the Vietnam War, THAT precisely describes our contemporary confusion: to deal with the Iraq War, we need entertainment more gory than ever before. Apparently. Again, as if there was no alternative. THAT is the greatest trick of the light of the angel's diabolic counterparts: that we now accept horror as part of our human condition. It has not only become a best-selling export article of Hollywood, but consumers all over the planet have accepted it as legitimate food for the eyes and the mind. In a way, you could say that the violence-driven pop culture has dragged us into the same pit of stupor that Osama bin Laden pulled us into. And we've gotten used to both. Fear rules! Blood rules. Not only in the news but also in movies and other popular cultures.

Mary: Yes, there's a desire for this kind of violence, partly because we have yet to find the language to deal with violence – I guess that's what we are exploring ... So, how do we provide the thrill – the excitement, the inspiration, if you like – without fear? Since fear really is the basis of so much of what we do and feel. Whether it is in our own personal lives or in the broader social and political landscapes.

Wim: That's exactly the entry question to the twenty-first century: What is the password, the code, so to speak, to replace and eliminate the attraction of fear? And I have no other approach to an answer than to refer back to the angels. And to look at not what they are messengers OF, but WHO they are messengers FOR. As messengers, they must be a link to the sender of messages. Their whole being implies that they are to serve as go-betweens, and not to take themselves too seriously. The medium, in this case, is definitely not the message. So for me, as a Christian, I don't even have to believe in angels, as long as I can just take them for the metaphor of the message they are delivering. And for me that all-important, fear-shattering, utmost inspiring and exciting recognition is that there is a God who cares. That we are loved, after all. Of course, that changes everything. I don't even have to explain myself any further, I suppose. What could provide greater thrill? And I feel myself in line with other people of faith. Buddhists, Jews, Hindus . . . Muslims as well; after all, I know that Islam is not a religion that in any way would indict or promote fear or hate, or prescribe the destruction of the non-believers. It is just that medieval concept of religion paired with the worldly power of 'government' that wreaks havoc. That sort of fundamentalism has always created terrible collateral damage. Anywhere. Anytime.

But to come back to your question: How could I share that excitement and that inspiration with people for whom a loving God is inconceivable? What is the other common platform on which we can conspire against fear? What could help us promote the absence of fear?

As I see it, we need a consolidated and massive new approach to inequality. Every person in the 'First World' becomes responsible for one person in the 'Third World'. Every politician in our Western civilisation spends three months in one of the ten poorest countries of the world. Every youth who's supposed to do military service in his or her country can spend the same amount of time on a humanitarian project anywhere in the world. If more people from 'rich countries' actually knew the living conditions in poor countries, the world would be better off.

*

Mary: There's a good quote from the Qur'an that reflects what you are saying about faith: 'The servants of the Lord of Mercy are those who walk humbly on the earth, and who, when the foolish address them, reply, "Peace"!' (25:63). And I reckon that joy, and compassion are equally – if not more so – our natural state of being in the world. These are the conditions for true love and faith.

Wim: YES! Looking into the eyes of children, anywhere in the world, I would say that joy, trust, compassion, absence of fear and so on, are the initial natural ingredients of any human being on this planet.

Mary: Yes, I think loving compassion as well as mercy – which is part of the spiritual realm which angels occupy – is to travel in this direction? To find real 'heart', so to speak, is what we need …

Wim: Absolutely. And I am convinced that the vast majority of people all over the world want to get to that place. What keeps us from doing it? Let's study that question for a while! In the end, you'll realise that most people are afraid to lose what they have. And the richer you are, the more you have to lose, and the more you have to hold on to things. The entities in our present world who are holding on to what they have in the most rigid way are the Big Corporations. PEOPLE can deal with possessions, and the idea of having to share them. Corporations cannot. The biggest stumbling blocks on the way to Civilisation, to the 'absence of fear', are those international conglomerates (check out the movie with that title: *The Corporation*). They definitely don't want to find 'heart'. They cannot even know what it is. They are scared shitless, all the time. That's most obvious when they make their goodwill campaigns and show us in expensive advertisements how much they care, for the Earth, for the waters, for the forests, for the animals.

Mary: I read something very lovely about fear: the heart is to the mind what a mother is to a frightened child; I think such a compassionate embrace toward others and ourselves could help transcend fear.

Wim: That certainly feels nice and comfy. But what about the scared heart that finds solace only when something finally makes sense to the mind. The child that listens to a good night story is soothed because that story, whatever it is, creates some sort of sense. That's what our basic need for stories is all about: They give us the feeling that the world is governed by underlying principles. In a way, I always found philosophy soothing. What I want to say is: Do not to underestimate the healing power of stories and thoughts.

Mary: I think that what you are doing may be finding that ethical embrace?

Wim: Maybe. My work, over the years, taught me a few things. Nothing is worth anything, in the long run, that is not done with love and conviction. And you don't have to convince anybody other than yourself before you address others. With love it's the same thing: if you don't respect yourself, you won't appreciate others. I'm not sure that this is an appropriate answer to your question. But maybe I was trying to define 'embrace', just for myself...

*

beatitudes

May 2004

Dear Wim,

I've been thinking about poverty and inequality and homelessness of late. In our last correspondence, you talked about poverty and inequality. I want to tell you of an encounter I had recently that reminds me of poverty and everyday fear and alienation ... in a slightly different way.

I told you of my mother's death – which reconnected me with your work on angels. But my brother also died last year. And here's the link. Last week I went for my regular morning walk to get coffee and bread from my local bakery. Over the last few years, there have been two brothers – who mostly live on the streets – hanging around this bakery (which doubles as a coffee house). The bakery gives the brothers coffee and bread, sometimes cigarettes and cans of Coke, depending on what they want and what is on offer on that particular day.

The two brothers are immigrants, but I'm not exactly sure from which country, since they speak in many different tongues. They're roughly in their early fifties, and quite mad. They laugh, yell and scream – sometimes obscenities, but often thanks to someone giving them a free coffee, or to God, or to whomever else they see in front of them – those others we simply don't see (this is a world of images we rarely have access to, and I'm starting to think the 'mad' have these images and premonitions that are very real and legitimate, but simply don't fit our reasoned world or we don't know how to communicate with them).

Anyway, this particular morning, I see Marion, one of the brothers, sitting on the street bench with his coffee and cakes (I know Marion sounds like a girl's name, but that's what he calls himself). As I enter the bakery, I notice that the woman behind the counter looks distressed. I've seen this woman for years and I still don't know her name. Then I notice there are some police heading toward Marion, I say to the woman in the bakery: 'I hope they don't harass him, you know – he's sitting quietly, having his breakfast ...'

She tells me that his brother died the day before.

He had fallen into Sydney Harbour and drowned. That's all she could make of Marion's description. Perhaps the police were there to ask him questions about his death?

We take note that they walk past him and continue down the street. This is the first time the woman and I have exchanged anything more than good morning and thanks. She goes on to say how the brothers looked after each other – taking care of each other, and making sure that each other was *always* okay. My heart really sank at that moment. I thought, this guy who lives on the streets has lost his only solace in the world. No other family, it seems... What will become of him? His grief?

Nobody pays much attention to him – and I felt that his grief would go unnoticed too – just like he does...

And I'm guilty of this. I've walked past Marion and his brother for years. Occasionally I have acknowledged their presence, but most of the time I didn't want to get involved in the madness that circled them or their obvious situation. What might they take from me: my time, my sanity, my money? What surprised me was my own lack of generosity and compassion. But what struck me that day is that Marion and I had much in common: death and the unexpected loss of a brother. So after I have got my bread and coffee, I stop for the first time ever; I say to him: 'I'm sorry to hear about your brother,' but his face hasn't yet registered what I said or maybe he hadn't yet registered the grief. I ask him: 'Are you okay?', and he says, 'I've got money for the bus,' and taps his hip pocket. That signals some form of safety... Enough money to catch the bus... but I'm not sure where the bus will take him.

Sometimes I wonder what he makes of me and other strangers who may stop – in the fantasies and monsters that he fights every day in his mind, and on the street.

I'm retelling this story for a number of reasons. I think it says a lot about what's internal to us: the fear and panic of another's destitution... Homelessness, immigrants, refugees and all sorts of related peoples and situations remind us of our vulnerability, and our very selfish and conditioned response is often: What will they take away from me? People are scared 'shitless', as you say.

But most importantly, I think, it's the sadness the shopkeeper felt and what I felt for Marion that gave me the first glimpse of something else – a real human connection and humility where the tears I shed later in the day were not for myself, but for a universal experience of suffering.

It may sound simple, but maybe the recognition of this suffering – that someone else suffers too – may end some of the violence and alienation that confront us everyday...

This letter is more a rumination, but it does seem to relate to our working dialogue – in some strange way – and, of course, to aspects of your work already travelled.

Make it of it what you will!!

My best,

Mary

*

June 2004

Dear Mary,

I read your mail again as I'm sitting in this plane that takes me from Havana back to Los Angeles, via Mexico City. I was in Cuba for only three days, just a quick visit, but it was again a journey deep into History and Time. The people are so POOR there, lacking so much, and yet there is such joy of living, such nonchalance, such relaxedness. No complaints. Smiling faces wherever you look. And no beggars on the streets, no madmen, no homeless. In the rich city I am returning to, you cannot stop at any red light without people coming up to your car window rattling their coffee cups. 'The hunger capital of America.' A quick drive away from Beverly Hills.

I think more and more that there will be no greater task in this twenty-first century than to bridge that gap between the poor and the rich, between the informed and the uninformed, between those who know the resources and those who have no clue.

I read your story of the two brothers. I once met a hermit by the name of Mario. He was an Italian monk who lived in Lisbon, in the middle of the city, where the bishop had given him an abandoned church to live in. Mario had no voice. Some thugs had cut his throat once, he could only whisper. Without his faith, Mario would also have ended up on the streets, as a madman. Every Sunday, he opened his church for two hours, and the people of the neighbourhood would come in and bring him food, and he would read a mass for them, silently. Afterwards, he would lock the place up again to be alone for another seven days.

For the poor, the mad and the homeless, often enough, there is indeed no other comfort than a transcendental one. In the 'other life', they will reap the rewards for their deprivation here. In my socialist past, I had nothing but a sneer for those beliefs. Actually, they made me very angry, as they seemed only to postpone any approach to a solution of the problem of poverty and inequality. Today, I take those 'beatitudes' very seriously. And I do feel that some of these people out there in the street are truly protected and blessed. And Jesus Christ who announced those blessings was in a position to do so; he had the right to speak of poverty and deprivation. He WAS homeless and had no possessions whatsoever. Which is why most churches drive me crazy today. They betray the very core of their own message every day.

Why am I speaking about this? I was trying to imagine you and Marion (and I constantly try to come to terms with the life I am leading in spite of everything I know and feel today). I thought of your tears, for Marion as much as for your brother, probably. Myself, I only learned to cry about the loss of my little brother years later. He was thirty-nine when he died, and I was forty-five. He was a radiologist, specialised in brain scans for tumour patients, and he died of a brain tumour. My father died five months later. He was a surgeon specialised in stomach and intestinal cancer, and that's what HE was dying from. I always thought of their deaths as if they had been soldiers who had died in the field. They had died on their own battlegrounds.

There is certainly no THINKING ABOUT PEACE today that can be detached from a THINKING ABOUT POVERTY. And there is no valid thinking, PERIOD, that has not known suffering. When I hear people display their opinions and I sense they are not backed up by the experience of suffering or at least by the empathy for it, I cannot follow any more. Compassion is the key and the password to any serious work. But who am I telling this to? And why?

All my best,

Wim

*

September 2004

Dear Wim,

I was driving home after teaching a class on 'evil' – and not thinking that much . . . I was driving up an onerous stretch of mountain highway and trying to focus on what I was doing, rather than the debris of the day and the effects of evil . . .

By chance on the radio I heard the blues singer Paul Jeremiah (I think that's his last name) singing, crooning, really, 'the world is evil at its core' – well, that's how I heard it. He was doing that thing that some blues singers do so well: linking social injustice and the strength of religious soul and conviction. Somehow it made me think of Blind Willie Johnson (and your film *The Soul of a Man*). And, then I thought, 'evil' – how might we talk about that?

We spoke of fear. Fear as the biggest stumbling block for peace. And we were talking about belief, not necessarily religious, but some kind of faith in things: in the spiritual force of our lives, what is real yet mysterious, present and enduring.

But what about evil? It's directly related to fear, don't you think? Once we cast evil as the source of all that is wrong we do a massive injustice to peace, as there is no room to move. People 'rightly' make a claim to all that is considered wrong, so blame becomes easily manufactured and projected onto others...

But in Jeremiah's song, evil seems an appropriate word when we are talking about injustice and inequality in America. Yet, it seems to me that evil is constantly used as source of moral righteousness, as it is by the religious right in America (the most prime example is Bush). War then is the necessary justification – on all fronts. This point is not new.

What is evil? Particularly if we believe in love... as the source of all that is possible. How can we really speak of god or faith or trust now – if evil is often the 'diabolical' counterpart?

I think that's enough from me at the moment...

With all my best wishes,

Mary

*

Dear Mary,

Good to hear from you after such a long silence (mostly on my behalf). I just finished shooting the film I had been trying to do for years, a story I've been writing together with Sam Shepard called *Don't Come Knocking*. And then my last film, *Land of Plenty*, about poverty and paranoia in the US, is just coming out everywhere (except, of course, in America) and I'm travelling a lot with it, talking to audiences and press about it.

EVIL. With my Catholic education and upbringing, the devil was very present, only that I never believed in him (her?) for a second. Even as a little boy I sensed he/she/it was more like a metaphor or a tool to scare people. It left me defenceless against all kinds of films, for instance, which showed 'evil impersonated', like horror movies. I still can't watch those. Seeing THE EVIL or SATAN appear (and they both were very popular in the Eighties and Nineties) makes me physically sick.

I guess I'm utterly convinced that THE DEVIL is only the absence of GOD, and that EVIL is the absence of GOOD, just as FEAR is strictly the absence of LOVE. Does that make a difference? I think so. If 'evil' is the absence of 'good', we know what to fight EVIL with. With unconditional GOOD. Other than Bush's politics. As he has actually spotted 'evil' and located it in Iraq (later on we'll find out it was all baloney...), he is fighting it with his best weapon, which he calls FREEDOM. I can't stand him using the word, knowing he means something altogether different, as only another reason for WAR. He says, like so many before him: 'War is good, if it is used against evil.' That worked when America entered World War Two; it didn't work in Vietnam, and it certainly won't work this time. It's just too obvious a disguise for greed. He and his warlords didn't even try to put up any disguise. When they took Baghdad, the army immediately protected the oil ministry, while it left museums unguarded against looters. How uncivilised can you get? And what more do people need in order for them to see the nature of this 'freedom war'?

I'm getting carried away. If the world was evil at its core, good would have never had a chance to show up. Good would have been unthinkable. Good cannot be a perversion of evil. That only works the other way round. For our subject PEACE, I mean: WAR is the perversion of peace.

All my best,

Wim

*

> Great Carthage waged three wars.
> It was still powerful after the first,
> still inhabitable after the second.
> It was no longer to be found after the third.
>
> Das grosse Karthago führte drei Kriege.
> Es war noch mächtig nach dem ersten,
> noch bewohnbar nach dem zweiten.
> Es war nicht mehr auffindbar nach dem dritten.
>
> Bertolt Brecht[1]

November, 2004.

Dear Wim,

I've recently seen Charles Chaplin's 1940 film *The Great Dictator*. I think the film's ending offers one of the most powerful cinematic instances for hope and peace.

As you know, the film is about a fictional dictator ... Chaplin plays two roles: the Jewish Barber and the Great Dictator – Adenoid Hynkel. In a case of mistaken identity, the Jewish Barber makes a speech as the 'dictator' in front of thousands of people in the dictator's newly occupied territory.

In the last minutes of the film, the dictator/barber characters become Chaplin himself speaking to us, to the world. He asks us to consider an alternative response to war and greed. Things may have changed since Chaplin's film: the acceleration of technology and war arsenals, but his words still resonate today.

I copy out the main part of the speech for you. It reminds me of some of the ethical questions and ideas of peace we are thinking about …

All my best,

Mary

the concluding speech of The Great Dictator

I'm sorry, but I don't want to be an emperor. That's not my business. I don't want to rule or conquer anyone. I should like to help everyone – if possible – Jew, Gentile – black men – white.

We all want to help one another. Human beings are like that. We want to live by each other's happiness – not by each other's misery. We don't want to hate and despise one another. In this world there is room for everyone. And the good earth is rich and can provide for everyone.

The way of life can be free and beautiful, but we have lost the way. Greed has poisoned men's souls – has barricaded the world with hate – has goose-stepped us into misery and bloodshed. We have developed speed, but we have shut ourselves in. Machinery that gives abundance has left us in want. Our knowledge has made us cynical; our cleverness, hard and unkind. We think too much and feel too little. More than machinery we need humanity. More than cleverness, we need kindness and gentleness. Without these qualities, life will be violent and all will be lost.

The aeroplane and the radio have brought us closer together. The very nature of these things cries out for the goodness in men – cries out for universal brotherhood – for the unity of us all. Even now my voice is reaching millions throughout the world – millions of despairing men, women and little children – victims of a system that makes men torture and imprison innocent people. To those who hear me, I say: 'Do not despair.' The misery that has come upon us is but the passing of greed – the bitterness of men who fear the way of human progress. The hate of men will pass, and dictators die, and the power they took from the people will return to the people. And so long as men die, liberty will never perish.

Soldiers! Don't give yourselves to these brutes – who despise you – enslave you – who regiment your lives – tell you what to do – what to think and what to feel! Who drill you – diet you – treat you like cattle and use you as canon fodder. Don't give yourselves to these unnatural men – machine men with machine minds and machine hearts! You are not machines! You are men! With the love of humanity in your hearts! Don't hate! Only the unloved hate – the unloved and the unnatural!

Soldiers! Don't fight for slavery! Fight for liberty! In the seventeenth chapter of St Luke, it is written that the kingdom of God is within man – not one man nor a group of men, but in all men! In you! You, the people, have the power to make this life free and beautiful – to make this life a wonderful adventure. Then – in the name of democracy – let us use that power – let us unite. Let us fight for a new world – a decent world that will give men a chance to work – that will give youth a future and old age a security.

By the promise of these things, brutes have risen to power. But they lie! They do not fulfil that promise. They never will! Dictators free themselves but they enslave the people. Now let us fight to free the world – to do away with national barriers – to do away with greed, with hate and intolerance. Let us fight for a world of reason – a world where science and progress will lead to the happiness of us all. Soldiers, in the name of democracy, let us unite![2]

*

land of plenty

Mary: This discussion took place in early 2006. Wim had already completed his films *Land of Plenty* in 2004 and *Don't Come Knocking* in 2005. I had recently seen *Land of Plenty*. It was Wim's response to 9/11 and America of the time; it is almost like an open letter to the country and to the events of that period.

The film's title comes from Leonard Cohen's song of the same name:

the land of plenty

Don't really have the courage
To stand where I must stand.
Don't really have the temperament
To lend a helping hand.
Don't really know who sent me
To raise my voice and say:
May the lights in The Land of Plenty
Shine on the truth some day.

I don't know why I've come here,
Knowing as I do,
What you really think of me,
What I really think of you.

For the millions in a prison
That wealth has set apart –
For the Christ who has not risen,
From the caverns of the heart –

For the innermost decision
That we cannot but obey –
For what's left of our religion,
I lift my voice and pray:
May the lights in The Land of Plenty
Shine on the truth some day.

I know I said I'd meet you,
I'd meet you at the store,
But I can't buy it, baby.
I can't buy it any more.

And I don't really know who sent me,
To raise my voice and say:
May the lights in The Land of Plenty
Shine on the truth some day.

January 2006

Mary: Recently I had the pleasure of seeing *Land of Plenty*; the DVD has been released in Australia. All good things take their time, I remember you saying ...

Wim: But sometimes they take too long to remain good. That film was meant to be seen *immediately*. It had a very short consumption date, so to speak. Well, at least that's what I thought when I shot it. I wanted it to come out before the elections in America! (And of course, it would have changed everything!) But maybe that's just in my mind, and I have to look at the film now as something that will have a longer life, and might act differently to the way I figured. It is definitely a film made out of IDEAS, but also made strictly from THE GUTS. (That in itself is a strange contradiction already, isn't it?) Anyway, those ideas and those guts wanted to act FAST and not take their time at all. (I wrote the story in three days, we wrote the script then in three weeks, and before we knew it, we were already shooting, for a very short three weeks, too. Our budget couldn't stretch the schedule longer.) Now the film is three years old, it didn't have the short-term impact I wanted it to have, but it seems to have a long-term emotional impact on a lot of people. So it goes to show that you can't trust the director's impulses. Some good things definitely take their own time, no matter how much you're trying to push them.

Mary: This letter may take you back in time – two years, in fact. But, only just having seen the film, it's fresh in my mind. So I'd like to talk more about it.

Wim: It's not that YOU take me back in time, Mary, or THINKING of the film. What's painful to me is to realise that the very ideas that the film is promoting have gone down the drain. History has continued IN THE WRONG DIRECTION – that's what's killing me ... Poverty and paranoia have rather increased since the summer of 2003, when we made the film. And the HEALING that the film is talking about has not taken place. Even the longing for TRUTH that Leonard Cohen is singing about in the title song *Land of Plenty* has not become a powerful political force; it keeps being drowned in more and more lies.

Mary: I find it a most absorbing movie and I am surprised by its subtle yet poignant 'political' nature. (It's striking to me how carefully it shows a particular reality, without whacking me over the head with ideology or opinionated positions.) It places the questions of human truth, estrangement and spirituality at the core. It's a very strong film about the state of fear, betrayal, paranoia and the 'American Dream' that keeps turning into a nightmare . . .

Wim: I remember that the reason for making this film in the first place was sheer FURY, but that I also thought: 'Hey, that's not a good thing to let you be guided by.' And so I invented the second character, Paul (I started out with just Lana in mind . . .). I wanted to talk about America in a differentiated way. Just bashing it would have been not only too easy, but plain wrong. Only by understanding (and respecting) a man like Paul, I felt, I had a right to talk about Lana. And so the film became a dialogue between these two characters. 'America' and the 'American Dream' is defined by their distance in the beginning, and then again, at the end, by their proximity. They are a very unlikely couple, that's for sure, but 'reality' is so very unlikely today, too. The bigger the gap you have to overcome, the better your chance to reach a meaningful territory of some sort of authenticity. 'Opinions' are the greatest obstacle to thinking, I sometimes feel. I pray not to be opinionated any more. That's what most critics have to offer: opinion, ideology, judgement. My favourite story of all times about judgement is the one in the New Testament, when the Pharisees drag in that woman who has been caught in the act of adultery. They want to stone her. And they want to put Jesus on the spot. But he just looks down and draws something in the sand with his finger. (WHAT?!) Then he says: 'Let whoever is free of sin throw the first stone.' And they all leave, one by one . . . (THAT is a great story of peace!). When they're all gone, he looks up at the woman and asks her: 'Where is everybody? Well, if they're not condemning you, I'm not condemning you either. Go in peace . . .' If only we could make movies like that: look at the world, then close our eyes (or look down and draw something in the sand), speak from the heart and then look up again . . . If the 'American Dream' keeps turning into a nightmare, as you say, it's largely because there is this damn (fundamentalist) urge to divide the world into black and white instead of allowing all glorious shades of grey.

Mary: I'm taken by many of the scenes, the script, the story – the images and truth are far reaching without a sense of dogma, but rather understanding; that is, *a love for opposing views* that ultimately leads to the transformation of fear.

Wim: I like that strange expression you used: 'a love for opposing views' . . . If that pious American Christianity could only take more seriously that most radical thing Christ said: 'Love your enemy!' Wow! Imagine how THAT would change the world! Instead, they do the one thing their 'enemies' suggested for them to do in the first place: hate them back! Isn't it infuriating how thoughtless and dumb it was on behalf of the government of the most powerful nation of the world to fall for that cheap and disgusting provocation and DO EXACTLY what these fundamentalist terrorists WANTED THEM TO DO? Maybe that is the final nightmare to end the 'American Dream' once and for all: that the country has lost the ability to love (or at least to respect) the opposing view. Then again, that's what I fought for in *Land of Plenty*: to take that lack of tolerance that America displays these days not for a permanent trait, but for a passing aberration. Great American virtues have been hijacked, that's for sure, but let us not give up hope that they can be reinstalled.

Mary: Yes. Virtues of love and courage have to be renewed ... And I mean love here in that conflict and opposing points of view are often dealt with through hostility and violence, whereas the characters of Lana and Paul – two very different takes on American understanding in a post-9/11 climate – bring together how love can actually be part of the process of looking toward a future. Love in the most humane and humble sense.

Wim: To speak of LOVE in the context of the post-9/11 trauma is still a daring thing. It is as if the nation had excluded that option, which is an amazing phenomenon, considering how deeply the country is rooted in Christian thinking. You can witness a certain amount of schizophrenia in the American mind here: 'love' is a category for private relations, and for idealistic ideas, but not for political acts. But it's in politics, and nowhere else, that LOVE matters most! I still cannot grasp how the Republican machinery was able to pull off that dirty trick: tell people they had a good Christian as president, but have him betray all Christian principles of love, truth, compassion and solidarity with the poor and substitute them with hate, lies, greed and the right of the stronger. And, as you're talking of looking toward the future: my big and most anxious question in that direction is whether those parameters for national and international behaviour that the Bush administration has installed can ever be undone. Because if they cannot be erased or deleted, there will be no decent future for generations to come. And 'love' in the most humane and humble sense will only exist, in fact, as a private category. Isn't that a maddening prospect?

Mary: Since we are exploring peace, the last scene of the two characters being silent at the World Trade Center site, and just listening, is very moving. It seems to me, when connection is lost between people and the world, and when only estrangement is felt – that is, paranoia and fear – then silence and listening seem to be great moments of peace. It evokes the spiritual side of things.

Wim: 'Listening' is a peaceful act, that's true. Listening to the silence, the void, but more than that: listening to the other. Our civilisation is constantly diminishing the culture of listening, though. It seems to me that our capacities for listening are getting smaller and smaller. The general attention span for everything is cut down, that's for sure, but most of all for taking things in. We're led to answer or react or speak up right away. When I sit down with a young film editor, he or she doesn't want to first look at all the takes, they want to cut right away. Or they immediately go to fast-forward. Technology makes the act of waiting obsolete, anyway. There's too much to do in the first place, and too many options. So, who wants to listen? But in *Land of Plenty* it's that very act of listening that brings up the beginning of a healing process.

Mary: What I feel from watching your work, and hearing of its progression in the context of our 'mailversations' is: here we are, in 2006, we started this project at the beginning of the second Gulf War, and now we are living in the shadows of a new world . . .

Wim: Exactly. And it is not the new world we were imagining when the clocks turned midnight on 31 December 1999 and we all entered a new millennium. But one thing is for sure: we cannot pretend any longer that it is only the minds of a few crazed religious fanatics that detoured the world. Sure, they brought down the towers of the World Trade Center. But what really tore down the very towers of our civilisation was the way the 'Western World' reacted to the offence. Well, not the entire Western World, but a big part of it. THAT is what throws the bigger shadow over our world today.

Mary: So peace, to return to it . . . I feel hopeful at times, and then despairing at others . . . our day-to-day life makes it a challenge to sustain something called peace. And its portrayal in cinema is almost non-existent. I taught a course on war and peace last spring, and found it almost impossible to come up with images of peace – we could discuss it, but it seemed the most obvious ways to make reference to peace was through war. And my students kept saying peace was the other side of war. But it's not, is it?

Wim: I'd hate to think that peace was just the negation or the reversal of war! It's got to be the other way around! But then your students are right, too. Images of war impress so easily. They are so much more 'interesting' or 'gripping'. Peace is not. Well, it's not that peace is boring for most people, it's just that peaceful things don't make great news. Why does peace have such bad press? In *Wings of Desire*, the old character of Homer asks: 'Why is there no epic of peace?!' Which is a real question. And if you look at the history of literature (let alone the history of cinema) you'll find easily that disasters and wars and conflicts fill ten times more pages than tranquillity, harmony, serenity or contentedness. And in movies it is striking how many more evil characters (devils, monsters, witches, gangsters, crooks, killers etc.) have populated the big screen than all the 'good' forces combined. 'Images of peace'... They are indeed hard to find. Or better: they are easy to find, but hard to sell.

Mary: Peace is much broader than that – it has within it love and violence. It is not one thing or another, but perhaps contains all of them within itself. I think we are only led to believe that peace is the other side of war, because that's all we know. Certainly we can talk of individual peace and calm, the spiritual sense of it and more global dimensions of its possibility. But 'being peace' contains of all of this.

Wim: THAT is a great notion of 'peace': that it incorporates conflict! Maybe we just think of peace too much in an idealising (and therefore deadening) way. We want peace to exclude violence, to be just 'peaceful', cool, calm and collected. But what about letting it INCLUDE discord, tension, controversy etc. if only and as long as 'peace' remains the common denominator? The trouble with WAR is that it erodes such a dialectic vision of peace. War is a totalitarian notion, while peace, by definition, includes, as you said, 'the love for opposing views'.

Mary: Can images contain this peace? Can stories or films do so? Are poetry and painting the only true forms of peace where we can get closer to the truth?

Wim: It's easy for poetry to claim the territory of peace. Words can define the world in a nutshell. Images can't. They always lead to other images. There is a worldwide convention, an agreement, a pact, on what words mean, isn't there? (That's why contracts are made of words ...) Yet there is no accord whatsoever on what images mean. They don't 'mean', to begin with! They 'imply', 'suggest', 'hint' or whatever ... You can right away start a new conflict when you want to 'define' what images really mean. In a culture that is more and more image driven, where 'the word' loses its grip on all levels, it is no wonder that 'the truth' gets so fuzzy.

Mary: Or is peace simply getting closer to the truth in whatever medium we use ...? Whether that is spiritual or creative, individual or collective.

Wim: Hey, I like the way you get me thinking! Is WAR therefore a way to escape the truth, to avoid it, to hide it, to get around it? If THAT is the purpose of war, the Iraq War makes much more sense! War not as 'the continuation of politics through other means' but as the replacement of politics, as its antithesis ...

I can't help but quote Dr Martin Luther King. He was a great thinker indeed, which means a lover of the truth, and he put some of his thoughts into very simple words. 'Darkness cannot drive out darkness, only light can do that. Hate cannot drive out hate, only love can do that.' You could easily continue: lies cannot drive out lies, only truth can do that ... War cannot end war! Only peace can do that ... Wasn't it the greatest crime (or stupidity) of the young twenty-first century to declare a 'War on Terrorism'? In the line of our thinking here, doesn't it strike you how ridiculous that formula was — and is — how much of a self-fulfilling prophecy?

Mary: I'd like to think more about this, but *is it* too late to reflect on this land of plenty? For me it evokes the ideas of spirituality in a time of war ...

Wim: 'Spirituality', what does it mean if not an affirmation of our belief that there are things we cannot see? In war, however, everything is visible, especially the enemy. War by definition only deals with the visible (another reason why the formula 'War on Terror' is so ludicrous, brainless, unforgivable ... It has led to another 'War on guerilla fighters', and wasn't that paradox a tough enough lesson already in Vietnam?) Why did the Taliban destroy the giant Buddhas? To show their power over the invisible? Or to confess their fears of it? 'Spirituality in a time of war' must mean to defend the 'spirit' against the onslaught of the spiritless, only that they come from all sides this time! Let's get back to Dr Martin Luther King and his thought about darkness. We need light to fight the darkness! And that LIGHT cannot be used as a weapon against those in the darkness! That would only turn it into a deeper form of darkness. 'Light' is the opposite of darkness, and it needs to be used in the opposite way. And that's also why your students are wrong to think of peace as just the absence of war. Peace is more than that. Peace is the most serious denial of war as an option to deal with conflict. 'War cannot drive out war. Only peace can do that.' And peace, like the light, cannot be used as a weapon against the 'peaceless' (let's call terrorists that ...). That's why I always shrink at the expression 'peacekeeping forces'. Peace in itself has a different force of conviction. I wish I could define it better. My best image is still how Jesus looked down and drew in the sand with his finger. Peace is convincing. Peace is contagious. Peace starts with listening ...

July 2006

Dear Wim,

I want to begin with your last sentence: '*Peace starts with listening*' ... and as I'm writing this, outside my window a big, black, and extraordinarily large crow is struggling to pick a branch off a dead tree. The crow seems to radiate a unique and strange darkness in the winter light. Ah, the joys of winter! Crows, as you know, have such bad press. They are often the symbols of death, and in my Greek family – certainly for my father, and heightened after my mother's death – crows are the sign of bad luck ... If my father sees a crow (or any large black bird for that matter) in the backyard, he'll shuffle back inside – it reminds him of what he's lost and fears most: death. It's almost like a tragic Greek comedy.

What we fear is death, or what reminds us of the unknown and the *invisible*, but we constantly use images of death to perpetuate fear. And, if peace starts with listening, then the 'dark' has its place, too ... not as fear, but as something else (it seems to me that one of the greatest teachings of this life is that we shouldn't fear death, because death is an illusion of sorts – that is, we should learn how to live, how to die again and again in the positive and affirmation of *this* life).

I'm reminded of your reference to Martin Luther King – and that 'darkness cannot drive out darkness, only light can do that'. Gandhi said something similar about the truth and light. He said: 'In the midst of death life persists. In the midst of untruth, truth persists. In the midst of darkness light persists.' Indeed, violence leads to more violence, hatred to more hatred – it leaves little *time* to do anything else. And I think your aversion to the expression 'peacekeeping forces' suggests, for me, the inherent problem. That peace can also be used strategically – and, at times, for political gain. So peace isn't necessarily innocent ... in the games of war and peace.

If we are to find 'spirit' in this time of war in the affirmation of things that we cannot see – what drives life – then I think we need also to consider the darkness. It reminds me of a Buddhist story: a man has lost his keys, and the keys are lost somewhere inside his house. But he looks for the keys under a lamp post on the street outside. When asked why he's looking for his keys under the lamp post, the reply simply is: 'There is more light here.' We can often shine the light in the wrong place ... to avoid the darkness.

We've talked much about how in the movies there is a striking number of 'evil' characters etc., and not much really that works toward 'images' of peace ... Why? Because if we are to explore the dark places that we occupy every day, it would unsettle us (and it might suggest there are dark places inside ourselves too – not just inside others). It might suggest that life is precarious and uncertain ... and to maintain belief in things we cannot see would truly suggest a greater sense of the mystery of things.

So, when the old character of Homer asks in *Wings of Desire*, 'Why is there no epic of peace?' it is perhaps because peace would unsettle us – and we would actually have to confront darkness in a different way. We might have to 'look' in different places. Maybe this reality doesn't sell ...

*

There is so much that our recent correspondence triggers for me (excuse the war-like metaphor!) but language is so much defined by war metaphors. I suspect images might also be (in the very technology?). Imagine a language, for instance, that didn't use metaphors of war as the basis of its structuring of arguments and ideas.

I wonder what you might think of war metaphors and language in cinema as well as everyday use ... to shoot an image, for instance, and other types of cinematic language as well as the speed of images and so on ... Technology, as you recount in the editing room, makes the act of 'waiting' obsolete ...

I'm thinking about the films of the Japanese film director Yasujiro Ozu. I find Ozu's work fascinating in the age of *speed* and the over-saturation of images; when I watch his films over and over, I realise what a gift his images are to us. Slow. Precise. Real. I think that Ozu is the forerunner of peace: images that evoke sacredness and humanity. I know that Ozu has been a great influence on your work.

I have recently seen Ozu's *Toyko Story*. That film is still very fresh in my mind (and it may always be). It made me recognise the relations that I had with my family around my mother's death – as the death of the mother in the film is stripped of excess: it presents what is, and the script captures the intricacy of the filial relations. Without sentimentality, but with pathos that is true, present, real and universal. Ozu's image of the father made me 'see', I mean literally see my father and his grief in a different way. Ozu's work provides a different version of peace ... of listening, of love and virtue. It offers up a like a gift: the lesson of living.

I think we can discover the possibilities of *peace* in cinema through Ozu ...
With all my best wishes –

Mary

times for peace

Times for peace are:
In the middle of the night
In the darkest hour
At the break of dawn
At sunrise
Early in the morning
All morning long
Later in the morning
During the day
In broad day light
At high noon
In the middle of the day
Early in the afternoon
In the sunny afternoon
Later in the afternoon
At dusk
At sunset
When night falls
In the evening
Late in the evening
At night
At midnight
Late at night
and so on.

Open-air Screen, Palermo, Italy, 2007
(Wim Wenders)

> One comes not into a world but into a question.
> Emmanuel Levinas

2

Inventing Peace

In this chapter, we reframe the question 'What is peace?' to move beyond the dialectic of war and peace in our habits of mind and culture, as well as to establish a dialogical relationship – the time and place of peace in our thinking and writing. And in our *dia-flow* of writing we consider some methods or techniques for inventing peace.

Peace requires inventing. What else could 'inventing' mean here than the creation of something new. Usually war and peace are seen as the opposite of each other, there is either war or peace. In many ways, we can hear the echo of George Orwell, when he astutely wrote that the great propaganda machines of the twentieth century have claimed war as peace and peace as war.[1] We can say that it is even more amplified in the twenty-first century. Perhaps the greatest obstacle to peace is the fear of peace – that is, there is a fear of uncertainty, since most of us have no adequate moral or visual vocabulary for peace.

German author Bertolt Brecht captures this absurdity of war and peace in his 1939 play *Mother Courage and her Children*:

> **Sergeant:** It's too long since they had a war here; stands to reason. Where's their sense of morality to come from? Peace – that's just a mess; takes war to restore order. Peacetime, the human race runs wild. People and cattle get buggered, who cares? . . . I've been in places ain't seen war for nigh seventy years: folks hadn't got names, couldn't tell one another apart. Takes a war to get proper nominal rolls and inventories – shoes in bundles and corn in bags, and man and beast properly numbered and carted off, cause it stands to reason: no order, no war.[2]

What Brecht captures so well is how war is valorised, and peace becomes subsumed under the moral advances and passions that war engenders. For instance, virtues such as courage, heroism, hope, trust are produced by the necessity of war not of peace, just as peace is most often understood as 'abstract' and inconceivable and war as real and inevitable. At the beginning of the twentieth century, the American philosopher and psychologist William James wrote that we need to find a 'moral equivalent of war', since all the passions and virtues of war outweigh any moral significance or virtue of peace.[3] Peace might be considered boring and uneventful in this light, as James suggests, we must 'foster rival excitements, and invent new outlets for heroic energy'.[4]

Moreover, James writes that humans have adapted themselves to war in such a way that it is ingrained in our very cellular memories. It is the embodied habits of memory and culture that dictate our reactions to threat and conflict: 'man lives *by* habits indeed, but what he lives *for* is thrills and excitements. The only relief from habit's tediousness is periodical excitement.'[5] And, as he perceptively notes:

> Man, biologically considered, and whatever else he may be into the bargain, is the most formidable of all beasts of prey, and, indeed the only one that preys systematically on his own species.[6]

Humans are the only species that has developed the systematic habits of war through its language and technologies. We must consider these habits to orchestrate change, because when we live in a world of habit, we lose sight of the fact that war and peace arise from a common source or problem – that is, how to address violence. We can say that the dialectic of war and peace tends to be the norm in our thinking and morality, but this is a badly stated problem.

In the early part of the twentieth century, French philosopher Henri Bergson wrote about the problem of human habits and perception in response to the scientific thinking and philosophy of his time.[7] Today, his writing gives us a method to consider this problem of war and peace. For Bergson, the problem of perception in a philosophical as well as an ordinary sense is that of badly stated questions or problems: humans tend to pose questions that assume 'correct' answers or absolute truths. So while it is necessary to acknowledge the dialectic structures of war and peace that frame so much of our cultural habits and perceptions of peace, rather than repeating these habits of mind and memory, we must pose new questions.

So how do we address the question of peace?

Bergson again offers some clues. For Bergson, all creative enterprise, all forms of invention, rest in the power to decide, to constitute problems in themselves; that is, to invent what did not exist. For Bergson, there is a difference between inventing and discovery. Discovery is what might already exist, actually or virtually, so it will happen sooner or later. We might say, then, to invent – as Bergson writes, 'gives being to what did not exist; it might never have happened'.[8]

To invent involves a creative impulse that arises from an open question, in this case: How do we invent peace? For Bergson, invention comes out of the creative potential of mind and memory. In essence, life is about energy and movement; the material world moves through a continual flow of time (duration), just as the mind inhabits the world of memory and imagination.[9] In this view, our individual lives are quintessentially embodied time, the creative flows and energies that arise out of the *real* as it is lived and actualised.

So all worldly experience exists in the realm of time that is indivisible. We are immersed in time that co-exists on different levels and planes of experience (that is, memories, feelings and habits), whether we perceive them or not. While Bergson offers us a good account of lived time, he does not fully account for the moments of 'interruption' that are states of relaxation, the moments between stillness and action – the flow or rhythm of another kind – that are the ground of being.

French philosopher Gaston Bachelard suggests that lived experience is composed of moments of stillness and action, just as it is composed of flow and movement. For Bachelard, change arises out of 'interruptions' in the flow of lived time: for instance, the conditions of repose – moments of reverie where there is stillness, an opening out of time and its density.[10] Reverie understood in this way is not daydream in the usual sense; reverie is the moment when thought and consciousness become pure states of observation and understanding. It is an awakening to the richness of reality and consciousness. Even more so, reverie is the imaginative potential of the human mind and the real that informs it.[11]

In this respect, Bachelard writes that matter is first dreamed and not perceived. Imagination comes out of the material world that we experience, not the other way around. Usually imagination is considered a collection of sense perceptions combined, but, for Bachelard, each moment has an imaginative potential to create and transform how we *look* at the world, because it is the world that speaks. In this potential, we can move between moments of stillness and action, of movement and perception. This potential can unite what may seem contrary, inexplicable or divisive in our perceptive habits. Bachelard writes,

> One dreams in front of his fire, and the imagination discovers that the fire is the motive force for a world. One dreams in front of a spring and the imagination discovers that water is the blood of the earth, that the earth has living depths.[12]

Inventing, then, arises out of a different understanding of time and space. This time is not clock time, but living time, the cycles and movements of life and death that are much like the seasons. In 'real time', change is inherent in every action, in every possibility. It is our habitual patterns of thinking that fragment time and immobilise it, so thinking becomes static and closed. A society that is closed in Bergson's view has limited morals and spiritual temperament.[13] We might say that a fragmented worldview separates and alienates us from each other, and in this alienation we lose sight of the uniqueness of each and every encounter in a more ecological state of mind.

Bergson offers a useful account of the *time* to invent, a method to help us pose questions about peace, just as he gives a sense of life's energy and flow in time and its potential mystery. Just as Bachelard invites us to consider the time and space of living that can transform the very act of seeing, he writes that every moment is fertile in its newness and difference, its poetry. Memory in its etymological shape invites us to consider the Latin *memor*, which suggests the presence of mind, so there is a certain depth in each moment, each moment is pregnant with experience.[14] It is in this quality of seeing that we move toward memory; with a certain presence of mind, we can look toward the past with grace as well as acceptance.

It is in this enduring quality of time that genuine experience and connectedness to the world can arise – Martin Buber calls this 'genuine dialogue' because it is in the *flow* of experience we are able to relate to each other and experience the world. As Buber notes, 'the present is not fugitive and transient, but continually present and enduring.'[15]

It is the enduring quality of time that moves us closer to the infinite, but, as Rainer Maria Rilke once noted, there is another world out there, but it is the same as this one.

once

In French filmmaker Chris Marker's 1983 film *Sans soleil*, he takes a look at the question of time and its legacies, borrowing from T.S. Eliot's beautiful poem 'Ash Wednesday'.[16] The English version of the film starts with the following epigraph:

> Because I know that time is always time
> And place is always and only place
> And what is actual is actual only for one time
> And only for one place.

Marker is fascinated by the actuality of time, the banality of living, the lying, the waiting, the snatches of life caught on ferry boats, as the film documents the journey of Japanese workers, as well as other people and places around the globe. The film's narrator speaks of the 'small fragments of war enshrined' in the daily habits of life, those of us 'waiting for a past or future war'. Marker takes note of how the colonisation of space was the preoccupation of the nineteenth century and how today it is *time* that is colonising space. We can say, as new information technologies circulate the globe at lightning speed, that our relations to time and space have radically altered. The world has become more and more fragmented, just as our quality of everyday life has changed how we see and experience the world. However, as T.S. Eliot reflects, it is the sacredness of time, moments between dying and birth, where time is irreducible, that matters most. For Eliot, each moment is sacred. He continues in 'Ash Wednesday':

> This is the time of tension between dying and birth
> The place of solitude where three dreams cross
> Between blue rocks
> But when the voices shaken from the yew-tree drift away
> Let the other yew be shaken and reply.
> Blessèd sister, holy mother, spirit of the fountain, spirit of the garden,
> Suffer us not to mock ourselves with falsehood
> Teach us to care and not to care
> Teach us to sit still
> Even among these rocks,
> Our peace in His will
> And even among these rocks
> Sister, mother
> And spirit of the river, spirit of the sea,
> Suffer me not to be separated
>
> And let my cry come unto Thee.[17]

Quintessentially, peace is about what is *actual*, is actual only for one time and *only* for one place, for it is in moments of time that ethical choices and moral implications of events transpire. The present is what matters. Reality, then, is: 'Inseparable, incomparable, irreducible, now, happening once only, it gazes upon me with an awesome look'.[18]

This awesome look is the threshold of peace.

*

But what happens when the present is seen as inconsequential, when there is no room to navigate the moral implications of a given moment? French filmmaker Robert Bresson demonstrates the moral restrictions in his films by drawing attention to what we do not ordinarily see in human relationships and their moral implications. His approach *shocks* us out of cultural habits of looking. He does this by reinventing the relationship between image and sound, what he calls 'cinematography' – as distinct from 'movies'. Cinematography is a 'writing with images in movement and with sounds';[19] movies, in his view, are only entertainment and noise. He saw all of his contemporary forms of media (television, radio, magazines) as schooling us in inattention and distraction (today we might add the internet and mobile technologies).

Bresson makes us notice small moments: an image or a sound – for instance, the close-up of the hands or the creak of a door. He highlights the 'fragments' of human action (the hands, sounds, silences) to amplify certain aspects of human behaviour and relationships, and in this amplification a new relationship to the image is formed. In many ways, this fragmentary approach is also truthful of historical conditions, since modernity has fragmented how we see, feel and think, but Bresson takes us one step further. For example, in his 1959 film *Pickpocket*, inspired by Fyodor Dostoyevsky's nineteenth-century classic *Crime and Punishment*, Bresson deftly uses close-ups of the main character's hands to demonstrate the 'crime' – that is, the desire and implications of this man's actions as he steals from others. The moral choices come out of the crime, not the other way around. Bresson's films bring together a different sense of unity and action.

Watching Bresson's films puts us in a *state of revolt*. His films often are unbearable to watch, as he demonstrates instances of human cruelty and 'evil', and the characters are crippled by a number of social or spiritual forces. What we often see is the indifference towards others when we turn away from the conditions that shape human reality; he focuses on what occurs when there is a loss of dignity and human spirit. Bresson said he was 'obsessed with reality'. Revolt in its original etymological sense means a turning, a turning around of events. In some ways the moral implications raised by Bresson in his films force us to look, even when we do not want to see.

This state of revolt demands that we change, and it poses the question, 'How are we to live?' in such situations – what can we bring to them? Bresson's 'revolt' may echo Albert Camus' notion of the necessity of revolt against the tyranny of injustice, just as much as the delusions of social rebellion.[20] The revolt of the artist comes out of the actuality of what is lived. We will return to Bresson and his 'cinematography' in later chapters.

One of the conditions of peace is to see. This seeing involves moving beyond the dialectical images of war and peace. But in the case of injustice that occurs time and again before us, we must learn *how to see*. To *really look* is to move beyond indifference and cruelty, just as much as it is about accepting human capacity for violence and evil. Bresson asks us to look at human evil and complicity in order to see the relationships in a new light, to help transform them.

Essentially, human destructiveness must be transformed through grace, mercy and justice. Novelist and painter John Berger writes that in the aftermath of the Hiroshima nuclear bombing and civilian responses to it, 'one of evil's principal modes of being is *looking beyond* (with indifference) that which is before the eyes.'[21]

What might it mean to *really look* at the world and our relations to it? Michel Serres states that we come into the world not through 'being' but through connection,[22] let us consider this connection, this question of looking ...

*

on a train of thought

The train leaves the station.
We go through endless suburban areas.
It is a sunny fall day in Australia.
Only a couple of days ago I left Berlin on a spring morning ...

As I stare out the window,
a thought comes to my mind
that has been hanging in the wings for a while,
and I finally invite it in.
It feels vaguely familiar ...
Where do I know it from?

When an oncoming train abruptly thunders through my field of vision,
I suddenly remember:
that idea first occurred to me in Havana!
I walked in the hot afternoon streets
and these packed buses kept driving by.
Those are quite unique vehicles, actually Russian trucks.

The Cubans call them 'camelos', as they have these strange humps ...
There were really lots of people cramped inside, sitting and standing,
some even hanging on for dear life in the open doors.
Some were reading, some were staring out the window,
and some of these looks included me for a split second.
They saw a passer-by who in turn caught glimpses of them ...

That's when the thought first crossed my mind,
or rather: came more to the surface:
'The world exists seven billion times,
in the eyes of each person alive!'

Each bus appeared in my view for a brief moment,
and I appeared just as briefly in the field of vision of a dozen passengers,
each of them perceiving me differently.

At that very same time
some of the other passengers looked at a line in a book,
or at the back of a passenger in front of them.
Others were dreaming (who knows what *they* saw?!),
and half a minute later
the next bus made the fleeting ceremony repeat itself.

I looked after another 'camelo' that disappeared in traffic
and then at that man in the middle of the street
for whom the world was his spinning oil drum,
and every now and then he looked up from it
to glance at tourists who might give him a coin for his trick ...
and NOW I was one of those, too, for a moment!

Now? The world was a permanent puzzle
put together simultaneously and continuously
by seven billion pairs of eyes!
And what a gigantic patchwork that was!

This realisation was quick and spur of the moment,
didn't really stick, then,
– or I did not pay much attention to it –
but the idea returned in other shapes and in other instances:

Among hundreds of people in the rain
crossing a busy intersection in Shinjuku, Tokyo,

and sticking out a head higher than everybody else ...
All these eyes rushing towards me,
hesitating for the slightest millisecond
and then looking straight on again,
while I was seeing all these faces floating by under their umbrellas.

Or facing a whole bunch of children in the Congo,
all staring with bright curious eyes at the stranger ...
And while I studied each of *their* faces,
they saw *me* from all sorts of angles,
actually from all around me, even in my back.

Or in a doctor's office in Berlin,
where all of us waiting patients threw glances at each other,
wondering about each other's diseases...
I tried to understand biographies,
decipher backgrounds and origins.
How did they see *me*?
And each other?!

The world is constantly fractured into billions of visions.
Every human being is another walking point of view,
every one unique, and permanently so,
solitary yet linked.
And every gaze is existing strictly in the now,
turning each and every moment into a memory
that is slowly fading as it becomes the past, behind,
and building up hopes and expectations for the future, ahead ...

Each single element of this world spectrum,
you right now,
me right now,
we all attach feelings and thoughts to what we see ...
Imagine the sum of all this,
this gargantuan kaleidoscope
of our entire human perception and awareness!
Seven billion pairs of eyes and the minds behind it!
What else should we call 'world'?

What else shall we call 'history'?
What else can we call 'memory'?
(I'm asking myself ...)

There can't be anything more complete
than the entirety of this permanent consciousness of mankind!

You can't tell me that it doesn't exist,
that this is a hypothetical entity.
What else exists?!
Every other definition of 'world' or 'history'
seems more fictitious, in comparison,
or at least much more abstract.
Seven billion people 'can't be wrong', so to speak.
Yet their simultaneous seeing, hearing, feeling, thinking, LIVING
doesn't seem to have much weight,
politically, economically and socially speaking.
They are a sleeping giant …

We speak of nations, or continents,
or the Third World (who's on First and on Second?),
religions, the Rich and the Poor,
North and South, Men and Women …
but we never think of ALL of us!
Why? Don't we have enough in common?

Isn't the common denominator of seven billion people
that they want to *live*, first of all,
and *in peace*, second of all?
And don't the two even go together in one breath?

~

As I am writing my thoughts about perception and peace down,
finally bringing these notions and questions to the surface
– or at least trying to take them seriously –
(still not sure what it all means)
I am riding on a westbound train across New South Wales.
Mary and I met in Sydney and we talked at length
about how the act of seeing and the desire for peace were related.
And also why had peace such a fuzzy image
and war such a clear and dominant one?
I promised to start writing on my train ride into the country.
Well, I have my laptop in front of me, typing ahead …

On the seat next to me sits this old lady.

She is quite small, frail and worn out.
Her skin looks like she smoked all her life.
Her eyes seem so troubled!
But she never looks up or over to the window seat where I sit.
She examines a whole bunch of newspaper ads,
the very kind of shopping flyers that I throw away immediately
when I buy a newspaper:
advertisements for cheap products like 'three for a dollar',
lump sales, dumping prices,
low-cost clothing, on-sale kitchen utensils and electric utilities ...
She has a big red marker and every now and then,
as she goes through these ads with the utmost attention,
she carefully and slowly paints a fat red tick next to a product.
Detergents, underpants, paper towels,
a hot water boiler for twelve dollars ...
(this one after some hesitation).

We share this space for a while.
I can't help being drawn into her choices.
Sometimes she is about to make a mark,
and then refrains from doing it.
Because she realises she doesn't need that item?
Because it is too expensive?
Eventually she rolls her flyers into one fat pack,
wraps a thick rubber band around it
(which she was wearing around her wrist)
and sticks the whole bunch into the back pocket of the seat in front of her.
Then she gets up and leaves down the aisle.
All the time she never looked at me.
She was totally unaware of me watching her from the side.
Who else exists in her universe?

She does not come back for quite some time ...
I try to get back to my train of thought.
It had started with the Cubans in the buses,
then I had drifted away.
Maybe I should concentrate on the idea of a universal perception.
That was the initial consideration and the driving force, after all,
the notion of an omnipresent and billion-splintered point of view
that forms 'the world'.
How then do these seven billion minds and pair of eyes
conceive of (and see) war and peace?

What can 'war' be in this context except the very sum
of all those infinite and unimaginable chains of traumatic visions
endured during 'wartimes'?
(By how many billions of people?!)
That total inheritance of mankind's worst memories,
I can only imagine it as a gigantic Pandora's Box,
which in turn must be feeding 'war'
(in our collective consciousness and in our genes)
as the inevitable and overpowering presence
that it has become in our civilisation . . .

Would 'peace' then be the analogue sum of all our gentle perceptions,
our good and soothing encounters and experiences,
hence the collected memory of a paradise lost?
Why paradise? And why would it be lost?

The seat next to me is still empty.
I follow the impulse to get up and go to the buffet car and get a cup of tea.
Walking through the train . . .
all these pairs of eyes again that stare at me!
(And all those as well that look somewhere else . . .)
I look into the gentle faces of Aboriginal people.
No other eyes I know are looking from so far back!
I can never forget how stunned and moved I was to hear for the first time
that in their own languages they don't have a word for 'war'.
There are a lot of elderly on the train, a lot of kids and youths.
I guess everybody else is taking cars . . .
Some of these people have that 'forlornness in time' around them
that hits me each time I'm in Australia,
and that I don't seem to see anywhere else. (Is that me?)

And then I meet 'my old lady' again, all of a sudden.
She is standing in the dark-bellowed corridor between two coaches,
shaking on the shifting metal floor,
looking at her right hand.
She is trembling.

As she looks at me without recognition she says faintly: 'I tripped over!'
And she shows me her hand.
On the back of it,
between all the dark spots and protruding veins,
there is a deep cut,

the skin gaping open.
But there is no blood coming out!
I don't know what we are both staring at with more astonishment:
the wound or the absence of blood.

I take her by the arm
(she moves like a feather!)
and slowly guide her to the buffet car,
where she timidly asks for a band aid.
The tired eyes of the overweight girl behind the counter,
seeing the two of us together ...
what an odd vision we must present to her!

The eyes of the Aboriginal people seeing me return to my seat ...
(That kaleidoscope again!)
I sit down and look at my notes so far.
And then I remember, finally,
that my vague idea of a multi-billion-fractured world view
once went a bit further.
It hit me then and hits me again now:
this sum of perception could be called
– I now call it – GOD'S perspective!
We perceive each other and the world *for* God, so to speak.
God looks at his (her) creation through all of our eyes!

If you're willing to follow my train of thought:
all of the people together in this train,
and what we witness, from a hundred angles,
and what everybody else perceives everywhere, simultaneously
(that woman hanging her laundry in her front yard right now,
looking over to our train rolling by!),
from a billion angles ...
WE see,
we ARE, collectively,
what GOD sees
right NOW.

If our eyes (and minds) represent a simultaneous 'awareness'
which constantly makes the world appear (and disappear),
then the very sum of all that can only exist
– and it *must* exist as such, I believe –
(and feel free, of course, to call that wishful thinking)

as part of the all-knowing, ever-presence of God.
That would make us God's instruments,
the 'projectionists' of his (or her) creation,
together shaping an ever-shifting moving image of the world,
a 'feedback' . . .

I keep staring out at the Australian countryside
in order not to miss a stretch of land
that nobody else might be looking at right now.
I smile at that sudden sense of responsibility . . .
But then, after all, isn't that the Aboriginal people's belief again?
Every one of them is responsible for his or her own piece of land,
has to keep singing it in order to keep it alive,
in fact has to keep *seeing it* . . .
The big difference, of course:
the Aboriginal people never conceived of the idea of 'owning the land',
they understand themselves strictly as the caretakers.
'WE' depend on the idea of owning.
Our entire civilisation is built on that principle.
We need to 'take possession' of everything:
ideas, objects, land, people . . .

And almost as if to prove that
I feel the itch, every now and then,
looking out at the fleeting scenery,
to lift my camera up to the eyes and take a picture.
(It has been lying next to me all the time . . .)
I keep the urge down,
conscious of how it reflects on the very context
I'm just dreamily pondering about.

But my restraint opens another can of worms,
and raises a question that has already bothered me before:
what might be the relation of 'recorded images' to the 'kaleidoscope',
to the big overall sum of every thing ever seen?
How much of the 'world' did the history of photography and film cover?
How much of it was 'captured', so to speak?
A completely hypothetical question, of course,
but certainly worth pondering about, I feel.
That could only be the tiniest percentage, couldn't it?
Then again, it must be an ever-increasing number!
There's whole cities in which each and every corner

is permanently under surveillance today.
On my iPad I just downloaded an application
that allows me to have live access
to countless permanently operating public cameras all over the planet.
Digitalisation changed all the rules of the game.
All previous ideas of perception have been made obsolete.
Benjamin and McLuhan could start from scratch ...

I turn my dazed thoughts
away from the endless gum trees passing by the train window
and to my beloved old Plaubel 6x7 camera in my lap.
Why I cherish photography so much –
that is, the (now old-fashioned) initial notion of photography
which is disappearing fast with the increasing digital picture-taking:
each and every single picture 'represented',
yes, in the very sense of the word, actually 'stood for'
a single, unique, unrepeatable instant,
a truthful glimpse from one person's existence
and into his (or her) point of view of the world.

Certainly each and every image revealed the eye behind the lens
(in the ever-present, invisible yet decipherable 'reverse angle'),
and often enough it showed other eyes looking into the camera:
tiny moments of the big kaleidoscope frozen in time,
caught on a strip of film negative
on which the trace of light served as a truthful witness ...
Well, especially that aspect of 'truth'
appears as a lost and nostalgic notion today.
'True' has become a four-letter-word in the context of digital photography.

It is important, though, to recognise a loss,
and not always believe we're constantly gaining competence.
Progress can also create deficits.
Let me explain what I mean:
some of the most amazing moments of humankind, in my imagination,
are those days in the lives of early pioneers of photography,
who discovered the very principles of their invention,
not only of capturing light and shadow through a lens
(that was already explored with the laterna magica),
but of fixating this fugitive impression on a support
that all of a sudden allowed them to preserve it!
The wonder! The sacrilege!

But at the same time: what a sacred act!

How shocked these guys must have been!
Here they were, stopping the relentless flow of time!
Freezing the ever-moving!
Saving the irredeemable!
And thereby rendering the INVISIBLE
(because that's what each image would have been a second later,
lost forever in the past,
if it hadn't been for that outrageous new act of 'photography')
VISIBLE,
over and over again,
and permanently so! Wow!
What an unbelievable step for mankind that was, too, Mister Armstrong.
(In my book that rates higher than stepping on the moon.)

We are taking this act of 'taking a picture' so much for granted
that the very idea of a sacred doing has gotten lost,
is definitely out of date, if not obsolete.
In my mind it still touches on the holy,
and is certainly still intact.
After all, we're messing around with the very nature of time …
We should still be scared.
(Funny how 'scared' and 'sacred' are just a typo away.
It happens every second time
that they come out the false way with me …)

Is there really still a 'sacred' base to photography today
or am I making things up?
Do I glorify the act by insisting to trace it back to its invention?

~

Across the aisle from me
a girl is going through her photos
on the little LCD screen on the back of the digital camera
that she got out of her backpack.
She flips through the pictures quickly,
and every now and then, with swift movements,
she deletes an image.
I recognise the familiar little symbols:
'Do you want to delete this picture? YES or NO.'

inventing peace

She seems to know exactly which moments she wants to eliminate…

Somehow that act of hers disturbs me.
The unique time capsule that each of her photographs represented
is forever rubbed out without a trace.
A while ago she saw something,
or lived a situation that she wanted to preserve,
which led to these pictures,
and now she is erasing that moment, for whatever reasons.
She is making her very own action of stopping time 'unhappen'…
So to speak.
At least she's destroying the proof of that.
So what?! Isn't that her damned right?
She didn't like it!
To delete an image, that's such an everyday act today…

I remember how horrified I was
when my friend Jim told me about visiting Robert Frank one day
and finding him in his kitchen, cutting apart his old negatives
with a pair of scissors,
convinced they should not survive him…
That was the same act!
The fact that it is now done by a button provided for the purpose
doesn't make it less violent than the scissors…

So why am I bothered?
Neither the girl nor Robert Frank
were really 'erasing', let alone 'destroying' time.
Time is indestructible.
What is it then that I still resent as an offence to time itself
in this act of deleting a digital photography or destroying a negative?
Why shouldn't we be able to simply reject a picture?
We made it, we can obliterate it, no?

Is it the uniqueness of each picture taken,
the fact that we saved that moment from oblivion,
that I cherish and defend?
Is TIME itself that SACRED thing
I'm trying to define here, after all,
with all my rambling thoughts?
Am I offended, so to speak, by a disregard of time,
by a certain careless disrespect,

that I somehow see symbolised in the 'delete' button?
I feel there is a crucial connection
between 'time', the 'act of seeing' and 'peace' here,
but I can't put my finger on it yet.

I've never been able to really think and visualise 'time'.
As a kid, seven or eight years old,
lying in bed and trying to sleep,
I broke out in tears when I thought about time.
The very notion of a beginning of time, or an end to it,
scared me to death.
I was lying there,
shaking and trembling from the (unbearable) notion of eternity.

Not all that much has changed since then.
'Time' appears just as unexplainable,
only that I'm not scared any more.
Along with everybody else,
I've gotten used to and come to accept time
as an inevitable and mysterious part of our lives.

As much as we've learned to control almost everything today,
we certainly have no control of time,
actually less and less so.
The more tools we own to supposedly save time,
the less time is at our disposal.
We are time's victims and its subjects, more and more so.

In photography, somehow,
we found a loophole to escape time, to detour it,
to make it wait for us or even 'come back',
so we can revisit it, when we look at a picture again.

My mother, looking right into my camera
with her wide-open scared eyes, weeks before she died!
Does this picture only move *me*,
because this is my mother?
Or don't we rather have to acknowledge
that *every* photograph is heart-breaking, by nature?
Each and every one?
Must be!
We only dropped the idea because, again, we got used to it.

inventing peace

Because we can't take the notion seriously any more,
that we are still committing a sacrilege,
not only when we take pictures of our mothers on their deathbeds,
but with every snapshot just the same.
Our intrusion, via photography, remains an infringement, each time,
some sort of violation of TIME,
a 'time out' of its sacred undisturbed flow.

For a moment I imagine the world without the invention of photography.
(And then film in its wake.)
What a difference that makes!
Things are only *there* if *we* are there!
If we want to see people, we have to actually go and see them.
We can't revert to any pictures, can't look them up and Google them,
show them to each other, send them or multiply them …
Memory plays a whole different part again …

Again, the Aboriginal people of the Mbantua tribe come to my mind
with whom I worked on *Until the End of the World*.
I could not show the finished film to them,
because some of their elders had died in the meantime.
When a person dies, they destroy all his (or her) belongings.
You certainly can't keep a picture of the dead ones,
or look at movies in which they appear.
Just drawing in the sand and letting the wind blow it away …

An impossible (and useless?) idea in our age, for sure,
since our world has long turned into (and finally become)
the BIG PICTURE OF THE WORLD.
There's no way to reverse that any more.
We have to accept to live with all these images, more so:
we have to learn to live more with the images of people and things
than with people and things themselves,
other than the Mbantua people …

~

The old lady never returned to her seat.
But we've stopped for a while already
at a station in the middle of nowhere.
I can't even make out the name.
People get up and start talking to each other.

'The train never stops here ...'
Instead, a train attendant now comes to look for the old lady's bag.
I make sure he packs her flyers and the red marker into it.
He leaves in a hurry.
I pull down the window and look out.
Further up the platform stands an ambulance,
a stretcher is just pushed into it.
The attendant turns the old lady's bag over to one of the medics,
then jumps back onto the train, which instantly starts moving again ...
We pass the ambulance, but the door is closed already.
I sit down again, shaken up.

I need to go back to square one:
How is perception related to peace?
I notice that each time the word 'peace' itself shows on my computer screen
– or in my mind when I try to concentrate on it –
I draw an emotional blank.
Why is that?
Why does 'peace', as soon as I try to think it or picture it
disappear right away in the abstract realm of 'desire', or 'ideas',
while 'war' immediately strikes me as real, when I evoke it,
as a fact, as a menace?!

War must have been utterly successful!
It has formed into a solid notion,
the sum of all its images, the BIG PICTURE OF WAR!

'Peace', however, somehow doesn't amount to a sum!
'There's no BIG PICTURE OF PEACE.'

That phrase just slipped out of my mind,
But I've already written it down and now I stare at it.
Why not?!
'Why wouldn't peace build up the same solid image?'
Can I explain that somehow?

I know the question well, though:
My character 'Homer' is asking it in a different way in *Wings of Desire*,
when the old man stares at images of horror from World War Two
in the library in Berlin,
with his guardian angel listening in on his thoughts ...
In the words of Peter Handke:

inventing peace

'Nobody has succeeded yet in singing an epic of peace.
What is it about peace that it does not create permanent enthusiasm,
and that makes it so hard to put it in a tale?' ...

I wish I had an answer!

Because 'peace' has never been durable in man's memory?
Because 'war' has better press, so to speak,
is more easily and so much more grippingly described,
offers conflict and heroism,
more glorious imagery, anyway,
than its modest counterpart, 'peace'?
I'm at a loss.

I stare out of the window, hoping for an answer.
Our train is now passing through some rolling hills.
Some big rocks are appearing,
sprinkled over the landscape like giant marbles.
The LAND is in peace, that's for sure, has always been!
Mountains and rivers and plains are here for 'an eternity' already,
they have not changed.
They exist in perfect peace.
It's men who brought the idea of war with them ...

It always strikes me in Australia, though,
– maybe because it is so distant from the rest of the planet –
how 'old' the land appears to me,
and how strangely calm and, yes, 'peace-full' it reflects the world.

The rocks become bigger,
they've turned into the foothills of a mountain range,
and suddenly we're going through some tunnels.
And for a split second,
in a sudden bright gap between two sets of darkness,
I see an old trailer home between eucalyptus trees,
laundry wafting on a line next to it,
on the doorstep a woman with a child on her lap,
both turning to look at the train.
Here they're seeing us!
And already we're back into the blackness ...
Another moment stored in that parallel universe
of time's very own memory bank

of everything ever perceived ...
(Considering the size of the universe
that little storage space isn't asking for too much ...
What do *we* know?!
If there are 'Black Holes',
why don't they preserve the reverse memory of our world:
everything lost and forgotten?)

~

I look across the aisle again.
That girl is still busy erasing
what she considers not precious enough,
all the 'stuff' that is stealing her memory space ...
I feel a bit guilty towards her.
I looked down at her innocent occupation
for the sake of some high-flying arguments ...
Who am I to maintain that digital picture-taking
can no longer be considered a 'sacred act',
or that the memory it creates is by nature a disappearing act?
Its main shortcoming is a galloping inflation (of many sorts),
and with that devaluation of seeing
(or any first-hand experience, for that matter)
comes an ever-increasing depreciation
of our notion of time being unique, precious and sanctified.
That thought must have been obvious to all of Daguerre's contemporaries,
while the girl across the aisle will not understand any more
what I'm talking about.

What *am* I talking about?
Am I still thinking in the context of 'peace' and 'perception'?
I am! I'm desperately trying to get to it,
to move into its direction.
But it is the widest field!
And on the way I'm getting side-tracked all the time.
Plus I'm constantly torn between what I *see* and what I *think* ...

I close my eyes and the thoughts run even wilder:
'In the beginning, in paradise,
when seeing was still innocent, there was perfect peace.
Until they ate from the tree of knowledge!'
'In nature, there still is only peace. All the time.

There is not even an antonym for it …'
'In the eyes of children as well: there can only be peace …
No child can have "the evil look" …'
'But what happens *then*, what changes it?
Why and when would it begin, the taste for possession,
the taste for greed, the taste for war?'
'What makes us lose sight of peace as we get older?!'

I open my eyes again and look at the empty seat of the old lady,
as if an answer was waiting there for me.
She was sitting there busily studying her paper.
Now she is lying in an ambulance
(silently staring at the ceiling? Watched by the intern?).
I still see her face so clearly.
The time we spent 'together', unbeknownst to her.
Our encounter in the dark …

Something is dawning on me,
and I hope I can somehow centre my thoughts on it,
something like a condition for peace,
when seeing and thinking go together, not separate ways.
I look around the train in order to grasp it.
The children that were shouting and crying
are now playing on a bench all by themselves.
The girl is reorganising her backpack.
Most of the Aboriginal people are sleeping.
The conductor is reading a book.
Outside, there's a vast horizon again, emptiness, gum trees …
We are all HERE!
And there IS peace, oh yeah,
inside of this train and outside …

Maybe that's it: when we are *with* the world,
with people, in their presence,
with things, in their presence,
with places, in their presence,
there is … an openness into which peace can enter,
a sort of … fullness of being,
a concord, an accord, a mutual agreement, a harmony.

However, when we are just with the *pictures* of things and people,
with their images instead,

there is void, longing, regret, anger ...
In short: absence of peace.
Does imagery have an inbuilt violence?
(Or rather: a magic that can turn into possessiveness,
power play, competition, conflict ...?)

The Amerindians' fear of being photographed
certainly came from a sense of protection.
They were afraid that something essential was stolen from them
that – once being photographed – would move away from them
into the picture ...
Peace is being *with* the things.
It is between people
when there is no picture, no stealing,
no violence, no possession, no superiority.

I remember when I last entered the United States,
the immigration officer didn't look at me at first.
He asked me to leave my fingerprints on the electronic scanner.
Then he told me to step back
so the automated camera could take a snapshot of me.
And only then, when he had my picture on his monitor,
he looked back and forth between me and the image of myself.
That's when the idea of the Amerindians' phobia of photography
came to my mind again
and made more sense than ever.
The man documented his power by reducing me to a picture.
I felt naked and at the mercy of this bureaucrat.

~

Months have passed since that train ride.
I continued writing on the way back to Sydney,
after visiting my painter friend Michael who lives in the bush.
I continued writing in the airplane back to Europe,
but when I got home I abandoned the text, at a loss with it,
as I felt I could not get to the bottom of this train of thought.

I'm not sure I can tie it together now.
I have a hunch that in order to appreciate PEACE,
and to be able to perceive it again,
we might have to move away from our culture of images,

and come back to the things themselves.
If ever that return, that homecoming, is possible!
Sometimes I feel
we have left the reality of people, things and places behind for good,
have accepted their disappearance
and moved on forever into the realm of their surrogates.

'Let's do away with images!
Let's get back to things!
Let's get back to people!
Unpictured, undocumented, uncontrolled . . .
If we leave things "in peace",
we might find the sense of it back ourselves.'
Is that a possible cure for our default perception?

How can we get in touch with the real treasure of mankind,
that fragmented sum of its entire kaleidoscope of peace?
How can we become part of it again?
Only if we can fathom that view, I feel,
can we get a perspective on peace again,
on the 'general good' of mankind,
the actual hope and need of our planet.
We are mostly too connected to countries,
ideologies, religions, economical issues
to feel ourselves part of the entire humankind . . .

Are we encountering the little old lady,
the girl with the backpack and the Aboriginal people too rarely?

Could it be that in the age of images
we completely overestimate its impact on one hand
and underestimate it on the other?
Are we misguided by our belief in them?
Like in the saying 'unable to see the forest through the trees'
we are unable to see peace through . . .
what?

*

love – between I and You

If peace is being *with* the world and others, how might we consider this 'withness' as an empirical question and a tool for change? Martin Buber writes that genuine responsibility for what we see and encounter in this world exists only when there is real responding to each other, for what happens to one, for what is seen, felt and heard. Genuine responsibility arises 'between man and man', but this relationship is not limited to the traffic between humans; it is about *becoming aware* of all things, the world as we encounter it and its sacredness. Buber writes:

> It by no means needs to be a man of whom I become aware. It can be an animal, a plant, a stone. No kind of appearance or event is fundamentally excluded from the series of things through which from time to time something is said to me. Nothing can refuse to be the vessel for the Word. The limits of the possibility of dialogue are the limits of awareness.[23]

Buber's account of becoming aware is to observe, and to observe has a special function in the sense of justice and equality, since to observe involves the whole of an experience, not just getting stuck in the fragments of what we see, our limited vision. Etymologically speaking, observe contains the word to 'serve'; service in this light is not exploitation, but humility and respect. Since we are concerned with inventing peace, we might say the service to reality is the only true function of peace.

Buber's notion of observation involves what we can call a 'whole experience'. We cannot be simply blinded or limited by partial vision and belief. We are reminded that the word 'whole' shares its etymological root with 'holy'. In this way, the whole (holy) invites us to see the uniqueness and sanctity of experience. Even more so: David Bohm suggests it is our habits of culture and mind that limit this understanding of wholeness (holiness) and unity, wholeness and the implicate order.[24] In Bohm's view, humans partake in the cosmos, but we have created a world of fragmentation that keeps us at a distance from understanding the unity of this kind – whether we call it a god or other qualities – it is certainly the realm of mystery and encounter.

For Buber, the greatest tragedy of modern life is the alienation experienced when we live in the realm of the *I–It* (Ich–Es) – the world of the ego and illusion, where people and things are turned into objects. Genuine experience exists in the realm of *I–You* (Ich–Du).[25] For Buber, the *I–You* relation is the primary word spoken between humans, but this dialogue may be silent and without words, for genuine dialogue is a response to what is addressed to us. We are *with* each other, not separated from the world; all real experience exists in the meetings and encounters we have in this world. And it is in these meetings that we enter the ethical realm.

The sphere of I–You is the invisible sphere that exists between us, it is like the eye that is awakened by light, the refractions of light and shadows that make the world and its objects visible to us. Light is an energy that moves and transforms, without light there would be no life or vision. The Genesis story attests this. Our vision then is made up of everything and nothing, just as the space between us is full and empty with potential. This sphere is made *visible* by becoming aware, by being attuned to the reality that exists between us, our lived encounter. But in the world of I–It there is a myopic vision and monologue that addresses only its own certitude and meaning. Buber states it this way:

> Primary words are spoken from the being.
> If *You* is said, the *I* of the combination *I–You* is said along with it.
> If *It* is said, the *I* of the combination *I–It* is said along with it.
> The primary word *I–You* can only be spoken with the whole being.
> The primary word *I–It* can never be spoken with the whole being.[26]

*

There is one filmmaker who depicts the primacy of this *I–You* relations in most of his films: the Japanese director Yasujiro Ozu. His films repeat similar storylines: his films are particularly Japanese in character and tone, but they are universal stories that embrace the *I–You* encounter. There is no 'point of view' in Ozu's films; in watching his films we do not objectify or even identify with any particular character – we are *with* all of his characters, we share their conflicts and dramas without judgement or contempt. This is a very special kind of observation.

In Ozu's approach to filmmaking, human relations in all their grace, humility and vulnerability are allowed to take shape before us. Through our *being with* his characters rather than objectifying or judging them, he invites a certain generosity and care. In this way, Ozu's films give a genuine hospitality towards others and ourselves – what the German philosopher Immanuel Kant only dreamed of when he wrote that universal hospitality between nations and peoples was the hallmark of eternal peace.[27] In Chapter 3 we will return to Ozu and these issues of hospitality and generosity, as well as Ozu's unique visual language and moral sensibility.

We can further extend the *I–You* relations, as it embraces the love that Ozu has for his characters, and what Buber calls a love that ranges beyond what we can say about it. It is neither sentimental nor romantic, but it is essentially the energy and attitude that is required for a caring look at reality. He writes:

> Love ranges in its effect through the whole world. In the eyes of him who takes his stand in love, and gazes out of it, men are cut free from their entanglement in bustling activity. Good people and evil, wise and foolish, beautiful and ugly, become successively real to him; that is, set free they step forth in their singleness, and confront him as *You* ...
> Love is a responsibility for an *I* for a *You*.[28]

And, as he writes,

> — You speak of love as though it were the only relation between men. But properly speaking, can you take it even only as an example, since there is such a thing as hate?
> — So long as love is 'blind', that is, so long as it does not see a *whole* being, it is not truly under the sway of the primary word of relation. Hate is by nature blind. Only a part of a being can be hated. He who sees a whole being and is compelled to reject it is no longer in the kingdom of hate, but is in that of human restriction of the power to say *You*. He finds himself unable to say the primary word to the other being confronting him. This word consistently involves an affirmation of the being addressed. He is therefore compelled to reject either the other or himself. At this barrier the entering on a relation recognises its relativity, and only simultaneously with this will the barrier be raised.
> Yet the man who straightforwardly hates is nearer to relation than the man without love or hate.[29]

To present a loving look involves respect and care for all that we encounter and see. It may seem radical or maybe foolish in the midst of chaos or tragedy, but in essence it is this gaze that opens out the freedom to invent, to make choices. And the power to make choices involves imagination, because even when we feel the most threatened, most hateful or isolated, there exists the power to invent peace.

*

inventing peace

a loving look

When I started to conceive of *Wings of Desire*,
with those guardian angels as the film's main heroes,
it opened up all sorts of questions.
'How do angels look?' was the most obvious one.
A much more delicate matter was: 'How do they see us?'!
How do 'we humans' look to them?

This was an important issue.
In a way, those angel characters were metaphors, anyway (at least initially),
an excuse to have a different view of Berlin
and of the people living there,
so their point of view was crucial.
How were they seeing us?
Critically? Full of pity? Mercilessly? Indifferently?
No, angels would look at us lovingly, of course . . .

This realisation quickly translated into the following problem:
'How can the camera produce a loving look?'
That issue became more and more poignant as we went along.
All the time Damiel and Cassiel were looking at people,
and we would shoot the reverse angle of what they were seeing,
and inevitably we were aware of the necessity
that our camera would have to somehow simulate their eyes.
Loving, gentle eyes . . .

Can a camera look at the world with affection?
(Or with any other feeling, hate, disgust, pity, anger. . .?)
We say: 'Beauty is in the eye of the beholder.'
Does that go for love and hate as well?
And what about the camera as the beholder?

The challenge, we soon realised,
was not so much to leave the loving look to a technical instrument,
but to 'invest it' into it in the first place.
WE, the makers, my camera department,
Henri Alekan as director of photography,
Agnès Godard as camera operator,
myself as director,
WE had to somehow endow the camera
with everything we wanted it to deliver.

In the film, children can see the angels, while grown-ups don't.
We told our little actors to look straight into the lens,
as if the camera was somebody they liked very much.
Some of them then smiled the sweetest smiles into the camera.
The 'loving look' thus worked both ways, it was reciprocal,
which only increased our responsibility and duty.
If we faked what we invested into the camera,
our instrument would in turn only fake its own 'loving look',
and it would also fool the children.
We had to double our efforts (and investments),
or our movie would strictly be Disneyland, cheap make believe.

Which had the strangest effect on our crew and on the shooting climate.
It was as if the angels we had called upon and evoked with our story
indeed showed up and offered their help.
(I couldn't help thinking they actually did.)
Ours became the gentlest movie set ever.
I never had a film on which so many things worked out miraculously.
In spite of the fact that we were shooting without a script,
our activities never became chaotic,
and problems always resolved themselves smoothly.
Once Solveig, who played our circus artist Marion
with whom the angel Damiel madly fell in love,
actually fell off the trapeze,
from about three metres high,
straight onto the stone floor, head down.
For a second the shock wave went through all of us watching.
She could have broken her neck!
Instead she got up, smiling,
and Laszlo, her teacher, got her back onto the rope.
The proverbial guardian angel wasn't proverbial at all, but quite effective.

I don't want you to think I'm going totally esoteric on you,
so I revert to a more worldly explanation:
Cameras only do what the eye(s) behind them do
(or tell them to do).
But they *do* reflect a very exact mirror image
of the emotion you empower them with.
The camera translates the attitude of the beholder,
his (or her) stance and approach.

That was a big lesson for me from *Wings of Desire*.

inventing peace

Well, not necessarily an entirely new discovery or revelation,
and you might be very well aware of this process, anyway.
The other thing I learned from that film was probably more remarkable:
The way we look at things does change them!

The loving look,
– the effort of it, the dedication to it, the purpose of it –
has an effect on what it is looking at.
The seeing has the capacity and power to change the seen.
In our context of peace and perception
that is most exciting.

*

faithful observation

Peace requires a loving look. For Russian filmmaker Andrei Tarkovsky, to observe reality with care and attention is the spiritual and artistic necessity of cinema. He writes, 'the cinema image . . . is basically observation of life's facts within time'.[30] In Tarkovsky's view, to be faithful to life's encounters is what matters in spiritual and artistic enterprise; once events or encounters are 'interpreted,' there is a loss of the uniqueness of experience, there is no genuine dialogue with the event. He writes:

> But one has to observe life at first hand, not to make do with banalities of a hollow counterfeit constructed for the sake of acting and of screen expressiveness. I think the truth of these remarks would be borne out if we were to ask our friends to tell us, for instance, of deaths which they themselves have witnessed: I'm sure we should be amazed by the details of those scenes, by the individual reactions of the people concerned, above all by the incongruity of it all – and, if I may use such an inappropriate term, by the expressiveness of those deaths . . .
>
> A group of soldiers is being lined up to be shot for treason in front of the ranks. They are waiting among the puddles by a hospital wall. It's autumn. They are ordered to take off their coats and boots. One of them spends a long time walking about among the puddles, in his socks which are full of holes, looking for a dry place to put down the coat and boots which a minute later he will no longer need.

Again. A man is run over by a tram and has his leg cut off. They prop him up against the wall of a house and he sits there, under the shameless gaze of a gawping crowd, and waits for the ambulance to arrive. Suddenly he can't bear it any longer, takes a handkerchief out of his pocket, and lays it over the stump of his leg.

Expressive, indeed.

Of course it's not a question of collecting real incidents of that kind as it were against a rainy day. What we are talking about is being faithful to the truth of the characters and circumstances rather than to the superficial appeal of an interpretation in 'images'.[31]

When Tarkovsky speaks of the incongruity of death and the examples of our response to the horrible and obscene, what he points to is a care and respect for what is witnessed. For Tarkovsky, the faithfulness of the image comes out of poetic means; poetry for him is the essential expression of reality. He speaks of the haiku as the essential form of the image. He writes, 'In a word, the image is not a certain *meaning*, expressed by the director, but an entire world reflected as in a drop of water.'[32]

Poetry in this sense gives the tools for a genuine dialogue with the world, its truth. We can hear the murmurs of the world, the speech of the wounded as well as the triumphant and free. In some ways, this sensibility offers a way to respond to violence without violence, but with care and respect for what is witnessed (we will return to this point in Chapter 4). With Tarkovsky's films there is a space for contemplation as well as a means to help us create what we see through a different lens of imagination and memory.

sacred means

What we have discussed thus far are the conditions that enable us to invent peace. These conditions are not utopian, nor do they seek an ideal world – they are present and enduring. These conditions arise out of the genuine need for dialogue. In this respect, they offer an artful approach to living, a creative attitude to life and its encounters. Inventing peace is method or technique in which to reconstitute how we see others and ourselves, just as it is in the inventing of ethical means to imagine the world differently. It is a sacred means to help redress the limits of our vision and the necessity of peace.

inventing peace

Martin Buber, when he was awarded the prestigious Peace Prize of the German Book Trade, spoke of what he called the 'Great Peace'. What he said was more astonishing if you consider the year was 1953 and the world was just at the brink of the Cold War. The following is an excerpt from that speech.

> The great peace is something essentially different from the absence of war.
> In an early mural in the town hall of Sienna the civic virtues are assembled. Worthy, and conscious of their worth, the women sit there, except one in their midst towers above the rest. This woman is marked not by dignity but rather by composed majesty. Three letters announce her name: Pax. She represents the great peace I have in mind. This peace does not signify that what men call war no longer exists now that it holds sway – that means too little to enable one to understand this serenity. Something new exists, now really exists, greater and mightier than war, greater and mightier even than war. Human passions flow into war as the waters into the sea, and war disposes of them as it likes. But these passions must enter into the great peace as ore into the fire that melts and transforms it. Peoples will then build with one another with more powerful zeal than they have ever destroyed one another.
> The Siennese painter had glimpsed the majesty of peace in his dream alone. He did not acquire the vision from historical reality, for it has never appeared there. What in history has been called peace has never, in fact, been aught other than an anxious or an illusory blissful pause between wars. But the womanly genius of the painter's dream is no mistress of interruptions but the queen of new and greater deeds.[33]

Cemetery in the City, Tokyo, Japan, 2008
(Wim Wenders)

All that lasts long is quiet.

Rainer Maria Rilke

3

Enduring Images

We devote this chapter to Japanese director Yasujiro Ozu. His films invite us to consider the ordinary and sacred elements of the everyday through his observation of human relationships and his unique visual and cinematic language. Unlike other filmmakers, Ozu touches most closely upon peace as being *with* others, giving us an ethical relationship and means to understand sorrow as well as joy. His films bring us closer to a sense of unity that inspires peace, as well as how meaning and value take shape through the social reality of the sacred, and its power.

mu 無

Ozu's gravestone has the simple word *mu* 無 inscribed; an aesthetic word, a spiritual practice, *mu* often translates as nothingness as well as emptiness, as Zen Buddhism suggests *nothing* is everything. We can see this aesthetic and spiritual principle in Ozu's approach to filmmaking as well as in his storytelling; although there are many aesthetic and cultural influences on his work, we will focus on the richness and austerity of his films.

Each of Ozu's films is a story of a Japanese family, yet every film has a universal feel and meaning. Ozu's films bear witness to the subtle shifts and changes in Japanese family life and filial obligations. His films are 'in the realm of the transcendental', they remind us of the perpetual continuation of life through the transformation and renewal of it, which is ultimately a creative affirmation of peace.

Many authors and filmmakers over the years have spoken of the spiritual and transcendental qualities in Ozu's film. In particular, American director Paul Schrader and American-born author Donald Richie have taken great care in showing these qualities;[1] in Schrader's case he writes that Ozu's films follow a universal style, a 'transcendental style': 'a style which has been used by various artists in diverse cultures to express the Holy ... The style is not intrinsically transcendental or religious, but it represents a way (a *tao*, in the broadest sense of the term)...'[2]

In our context, we suggest Ozu's work gives a method to invent peace through considering the changing but enduring qualities of human relationships – it is these qualities that put us in touch with the sacred as well as ordinary experience. His films are not high drama and action-packed entertainment, but through a careful film style he shows a compassion and kindness that is unique in the history of cinema.

Film directors such as Ozu, Robert Bresson, Andrei Tarkovsky, Carl Dreyer, Michelangelo Antonioni, Ingmar Bergman and others have each in their own way provided a film grammar, energy and style that shows the crisis of the human spirit and the need for sacred life. These directors' films and filmic styles are part of the history of cinema, but often their films are no longer decipherable to people today; their visual language has become obscure. Yet these directors' works endure because they find a means to express creatively the spiritual crises and alienation of our times.

However, when we speak of film grammar we are best reminded by what Ozu himself says: 'I don't think the film has a grammar ... I don't think film has but one form. If a good film results, then that film has created its own grammar.'³

autumnal moments

Ozu's film career, which spanned almost forty years from the late 1920s to the early 1960s, had one recurrent theme – the dissolution of the Japanese family and culture. Most often this theme was the pretext for all of his films.

Ozu's early silent films were often comedies as well as 'home dramas', most of the early films adhering to cinema of the day. His later films evolved through the keen observation of Japanese family life as well as the impact of America and the war on Japanese national culture. His films quietly document the changes in Japanese culture – for instance, a baseball cap on a child's head, a Rinso detergent packet placed on the floor or a Coca-Cola sign in the frame, every scene and object within it carefully orchestrated. It is said that on his deathbed Ozu made a comment to Kido Shiro, head of the Shockiku Cinema company with which Ozu made most of his films, 'Well, Mr Kido, it seems to be home drama to the last.'⁴

Through the home drama, Ozu's stories are like the cycle of the seasons; by repeating the same story time and again, but in different configurations, his stories show us something unique about family relationships. Most of his films resonate with the Buddhist traditions of the cycles of life and death; these cycles follow the seasons, each season returns, but each return is newly experienced. For instance, we see the general frame of *Tokyo Story* (made in 1953) already in his film *Brothers and Sisters of the Toda Family* from

1941 – the death of a parent brings to light the selfishness of family members and the legacies of loss and grief. And it is no accident that Ozu's post-war films and film titles often relate to the seasons – titles such as *Early Summer*, *The End of Summer*, *Early Spring*, *Late Spring*, *An Autumn Afternoon*, *Late Autumn* are like a haiku.[5] Each title distils a time and place of human encounters, the transience of life as well as its memory – as Gaston Bachelard might put it, 'the seasons of memory are eternal because they are faithful to the colours of the *first time* . . .'[6]

Ozu's films demonstrate the colours of the first time, moments of distillation of memory and culture as well as its poetry. The seasons of memory are immortalised, for instance, in *Late Spring*: at the end of the film the widowed father, played by Ozu's favourite actor Ryu Chishu, is slowly peeling a piece of fruit. In this moment we feel his aloneness; essentially, the scene distils the changing desires and loyalties of the widowed father and daughter in post-war Japan. In the last scene of *Tokyo Story*, we see this immortalisation again in the father (Ryu) silently fanning himself after the death of his wife. We will return to *Tokyo Story*.

Ozu's films are often spoken of in terms of *mono no aware*; this awareness relates to the pathos of life as well as its transience. *Mono no aware* has a long tradition in Zen and Japanese aesthetics, its meaning includes the sense of continuing balance of emotions and a gentle or 'sympathetic' awareness of life's transience. Ozu's stories convey a sense of 'nostalgic sadness connected with autumn and the vanishing of the world' that corresponds to the Buddhist use of *mono no aware* as 'this existence of ours as transient as autumn clouds'.[7] This sadness should not be confused with a longing for the past, but rather expresses the transience of life and its cycles. Although there has been some controversy in describing Ozu's films as *mono no aware*,[8] we suggest that Ozu makes us aware of how the present is *enduring*, the changes that take place in ordinary ways, the movements of love, loss and death.

In *The End of Summer*, there is a beautiful scene that speaks of life's transience with a man (Ryu) and his wife observing the crows that have come to rest nearby and the smoke that rises from the chimney at the local crematorium:

Man and his wife are fishing nearby a crematorium.
Wife: Aren't there a lot of crows today?
Man: Umm. Yes there are.
Wife: Someone must have died.
Man: Perhaps.
   But no smoke is rising from the crematorium chimney.
Wife: You're right.

Later

Wife: Hey, someone died after all.
   Smoke is rising.
Man: Yes, so it is.
Wife: It's pitiful if it's a younger person ... instead of someone old.
Man: Yes, but new lives ... successfully replace those that die.
Wife: Yes. How nature works.

They look at the chimney for a while in silence. Then continue fishing.

Ozu's stories unfold through narrational processes that are in real time: there is no jump-cutting, no quick advances, no compacting of time in a scene. In his films, there is only one time, the time of the scene. Often many of his film sequences directly correspond to the time it would take in real life to complete the scene, so as the characters experience film time, so do we. This unique cinematic time invites us to be *with* the characters.

Enforcing real time on us slows us down. It is this feature of Ozu's work that is lost in modern cinema. Ozu's films remind us of *being* in time, it is not clock time, but the rhythm and flow of life. His films are slow, his images are often compared to still lives, and because of this lack of 'action' audiences today may feel that the films are lacking cinematic purpose. However, it is in this enduring time – enduring corresponds to the sacred time we mentioned in Chapter 2 – that the present is not fugitive or transient, but continually present and expansive. Here we have the space to imagine, to reflect, to *become aware*.

For Ozu, the invariable wholeness of his work and the 'rightness' of characters comes out of stories that are *not* driven by plot and action, but by the humility and grace of characters as well as the trepidation that is experienced in different family roles and relationships. American psychologist James Hillman writes that trepidation is the first piece of compassion.[9] We see this most beautifully in *Tokyo Story* in the exchange between Tomi (elderly parent) and Noriko (Tomi's widowed daughter-in-law). Tomi is homeless in Tokyo, after family members through their self-absorption make their elderly parents unwelcome. Noriko invites her to stay; she is the only kin to show genuine hospitality.

Scene 111. *In the room, Tomi is preparing to go, putting on her tabi. Noriko comes in.*
Tomi: Thank you so much. I had a good night's sleep.
Noriko: That's good.
Tomi: But won't you be late for the office?

Noriko: No. I have quite enough time.
She goes over to a shelf and brings something back.
Noriko: I want you to take this. It isn't much.
Tomi: What is it?
Noriko: It's nothing, just a little something for you to spend.
Tomi: Oh, no —
Noriko: Please, Mother, do take it.
Tomi: But, you can't do this. No. It is I who should be giving you something.
Noriko: Now, please, Mother. Just take it. (*She forces it into her hands.*)
Tomi (*protesting*): No, no.
Noriko: Please.
Tomi: Must I? . . . Well, then. Thank you very, very much.
Noriko: It is nothing (*laughs*).
Tomi: You must need the money yourself, and yet you do something like this. I just don't know what to say, but (*takes her hand*), I do thank you, very much.
Noriko: Well, we should be going.
Tomi: Yes.
Noriko: And be sure to come here again, the next time you're in Tokyo.
Tomi: Thank you, but I'm afraid I won't be coming back. And you. I know you are busy, but do try and come to Onomichi.
Noriko: I really want to. If only it were a bit closer.
Tomi: You're right. It is far away.[10]

This small gift of money between Tomi and Noriko is a genuine exchange of gratitude and love. Noriko's hospitality shows a care that emerges between the characters, as well as the love Ozu has for his characters as a director (see Chapter 2). We witness the poverty of each character with compassion: Noriko lives in a cramped working-class environment, a boarding house; Tomi and her husband Shukichi live on frugal means as elderly people supporting themselves in post-war Japan; the trip to Tokyo would have been a major expense, a once-in-a-lifetime journey. Without judgement, Ozu demonstrates what otherwise would be taken for granted, how the lives of these characters are particular to their historical conditions and circumstance.

Noriko and Tomi clasping hands
(from *Tokyo Story*, 1953)

Ozu shows us the ugliness of his characters as well, with a certain rightness that is not judgemental, but more akin to the changes in family life and social structure. One poignant scene in *Tokyo Story* between Shige, the eldest daughter, and her parents demonstrates this 'right' tension. Tomi and Shukichi return earlier than scheduled from the Atami seaside resort that their children had sent them to. Shige is so ashamed of her parents in their country 'backwardness' that she does not refer to them as her parents on their return.

> Scene 92. *The Urara beauty parlor. Same day, late afternoon.*
> *Kiyo [assistant] is cleaning the machines. Shige is setting the hair of a woman who looks like a housewife. Another is under a dryer reading a magazine.*
> [...]
> *The old couple appear.*
> **Kiyo:** Welcome back.
> **Shukichi:** Well, we're back.
> **Shige:** Why have you come back so soon?
> **Tomi:** We just got here.
> **Shige:** You should have taken more time. What happened?
> *They go into the back room.*
> **Woman:** Who are they?
> **Shige:** Oh, just someone we know. Friends from the country.[11]

Invariably, instances of compassion are not just about depicting the 'good', the wholly good or bad; rather Ozu demonstrates human encounters without judgement. Ozu's observation of family life and its social decline are respectful. The issue then is not a moral judgement of the children, but we see the characters' vulnerability and humanness with respect and humility.

This morality corresponds with the construction of Ozu's scenes; for Ozu everything is in a scene: there is nothing hidden, there is nothing to be revealed, there is nothing wanting, nothing extraneous in his films. All of the detail is in the architecture and the (a)symmetry of the scene – the flow and movement of the film. In this way, it is *'what is'* in a scene that gives us a model for an ethical life. Rather than judging what is right or wrong in others in a more conventional moral framework, this ethical realm brings us closer to creating the foundations of peace, an ethical framework in which we can observe and openly relate to others without fear or judgement. It is this keen observation and openness that gives the 'right' response that moves out of self-centredness, fantasy or delusion.

This ethical realm is evident in Ozu's scripts, which distil the essential nature of his characters; his dialogue comes out of a basic storyline, not a narrative push that must be convinced by its own plot direction and action.

His films then have an inevitable freedom that may seem paradoxical, as the characters are often constrained in their emotional range, but it is precisely in this paradox that the dialogue and script are crystal clear in showing us the 'need although not a place for emotion'. We are not manipulated by the emotions or sentimentality in his films; the nuances of feeling and emotions are rather like a palette of colours, 'to render visible', as painter Paul Klee might put it, the world as it is.

Paul Schrader discusses the distinction well in terms of 'spiritual films' and 'religious films'; he writes of spiritual films as those films that relate to spiritual transformation or sacredness, and of religious films as those that seek an emotional realism that confirms a story line or 'religious' plot:

> The conventional religious film uses a style of identification ... the style amplifies the abundant artistic means inherent in motion pictures: the viewer is aided and encouraged in his desire to identify and empathize with character, plot, and setting. For an hour or two the viewer can become that suffering, saintly person on the screen; his personal problems, guilt and sin are absorbed by humane, noble, and purifying motives. The spiritual drama, like the romantic drama, becomes an escapist metaphor for the human drama. A confrontation between the human and spiritual is avoided ... It fulfils the viewer's fantasy that spirituality can be achieved vicariously; it is the direct result of his identification.[12]

In a similar way we can make the distinction between 'peace films' and films about war and peace. Films about war and peace want us to empathise with a character, plot or setting; they fulfil the viewer's fantasy of 'right and wrong' as well as a need for identification with the 'good guys'. Films that are organised around morally good or bad people or cultures – that is, good versus evil – do not necessarily change our habitual ways of looking, or our ethical relations with others. Ozu's films are unique, as they invite us to consider the ethical means and tools for peace.

Ozu cultivates a respectful treatment for everything that comes before the camera. Out of this respect comes the possibility of kindness; the French philosopher Emmanuel Levinas once wrote that 'kindness is the only morality'. Etymologically, 'kindness' links to the word 'kin', kin relates to the more common understanding of 'kinship' – ties of family and community – but 'kin' also refers to 'kindred spirit', the divine that is in all of us. It is with this kindness and loving detail that Ozu's films demonstrate to us something different and truthful about the world. Moreover, this kindness extends to the ongoing relationships he had with his actors and crew, most of whom worked with Ozu throughout his long career.

Ozu's cameraman, Yuharu Atsuta, speaks of this type of *kin* relations in Wim's film *Tokyo-Ga*, made in 1985. His documentary film is a homage to Ozu:

> My gratitude to Ozu continues to this very day. I was the caretaker of the camera. That was not meant as false modesty. I was proud to be the caretaker of Ozu's camera. All the more so because already as an assistant I'd come to know and admire him. At that time all other assistants had long become cameramen, I was still nothing but the assistant on Ozu's crew. One day he said to me, since you are going to be a cameraman sooner or later, why don't you be patient and become the door of a big house?
>
> I appreciated his words. Many of my colleagues were making more money, above all, the newsreel cameramen were very well paid. But I stayed where I was. I wanted to remain at Ozu's side. That was my view. [...]
>
> He left me in complete charge of the lighting. In the film *There Was a Father* there is a scene at the end. I lit the hospital room so it was extremely bright as if the sun was shining in it.
>
> In places like that, in a hospital, one is filled with compassion when it is lovely outside. So I had the sunlight pour into the room with great intensity.
>
> Ozu turned to me and said: 'Why, that's not bad, not bad at all.'
>
> And I replied: 'To be perfectly honest I did not want the old man to die in the dark. I wanted the old man to be surrounded by light at the moment of his death.'
>
> We shoot exactly like this, was the praise Ozu gave me. [...]
>
> I was quite fond of him. I had a special feeling for him right up to his death. And Ozu knew it. I know something like this might sound strange, but I'm probably the only cameraman in the world who remained with one single director for such an outrageous length of time. From assistant right through to the end. I don't think anyone else can make that claim.
>
> To have served Ozu, that's my pride and joy.
>
> Ozu got the best out of me. And I gave him my best ... I'm indebted to Ozu. Sometimes one feels lonely. Yes, one becomes lonely. What you call spirit that can never be explained to anyone else. The people he worked with he cared about. He was more than a director, he was like a king.
>
> Now at this moment he must be pleased.

Ryu Chishu at Ozu's Grave
(from *Tokyo-Ga*, 1985)

'Mu' – Ozu's Grave
(from *Tokyo-Ga*, 1985)

the lost paradise

If it had not been for an anonymous housewife from Brooklyn,
who at some time in the late Sixties
saw some obscure Japanese films in a local cultural institute
and loved them so much that she then went on a mission
and started sending letters to several American distributors
with the urgent call to action
that the American People absolutely needed to know these films
by a totally unknown Japanese director ...

and if it had not been for Dan Talbot and New Yorker Films
who actually then bought the rights to several of these films
and distributed them in art houses all over the country ...

and if I had not been told by a good friend
that I just had to go see any which one of these movies
by the (to me) mysterious director 'something Ozu' ...

and if I had not walked past the New Yorker Theatre one day,
recognised that name on the marquee
and aimlessly walked into the theatre
to watch this film called *Tokyo Story* by Yasujiro Ozu ...

... I would not have known
(and might never have)
that there once had existed
the (now lost) paradise of filmmaking.
Nothing less was my discovery that afternoon.
(And I can't thank that anonymous woman from Brooklyn enough!)

I didn't expect anything to begin with, of course.
For a while I just stared with disbelief at the screen.
And then I slowly started to realise and accept
that I was witnessing something extraordinary:
what I saw was what was there
and what was there was what I saw,
not less, not more.
Sheer presence, sheer truth, sheer existence.
Everything was familiar, yet so new ...
But I'm getting ahead of myself.

All I understood at the time was:
I was certainly following the most simple story,
– it's the same all over the world –
of fathers and mothers,
sons and daughters,
life and death.
But it was not so much the 'family story'
which gently unravelled on the screen
that caught me by surprise, and shock,
but *how* it showed itself to me,
and to that audience of a handful of people on the Upper West Side.

Not that I reflected any of this in that moment,
but watching the film I found myself calm down,
breathe slower, settle in myself, open up
and become part of this family on the screen,
and part of mankind.
'Father' Ryu Chishu was everybody's father,
and mine, too;
'mother' Higashiyama Chieko was everybody's mother,
and mine, too.
They were unique,
but universal and eternal at the same time,
utterly themselves
and yet the very image of their roles.

There was a rhythm on the screen
that totally became the rhythm of my attention and my heartbeat.
There was a simplicity and clarity
that made my own feelings simple and clear.
There was a modesty in each image
that made me forget the New York buzz of imagery outside.
There was a flowing of time that gave me utter confidence
that life was good,
that there was a purpose to everything,
if we would just enter that flow.

If ever there had been a paradise of filmmaking, here it was:
pure evidence, pure being,
pouring from shot to shot.
No plot was driving it,
only the necessity of human fate.

Peace entered my mind, my body and my soul,
a feeling I had never been exposed to in a movie theatre.

At the end of the film I walked out of the cinema in a state of bliss,
and at the next street corner I turned around
and went right back to see the film a second time.
Nothing changed.
On the contrary, I fell deeper into this peace
and experienced the steady flow of this eternal family story even fuller.

A 'paradise of filmmaking' meant:
we had been expelled from it, all of us,
and had started making (and watching) our films outside this realm,
in a hostile world,
in which such paradisiac peace
was nothing more than a utopian idea at best,
a distant memory, a vague hope.

In this cinematic heaven,
there was no difference between 'role' and 'actor' and 'viewer';
we were all part of the same life-story,
all on the same *Journey to Tokyo*,
our existences driven by the same forces.

How was that possible?
Both that we had lost that paradise
and that it had once existed?

I did not understand this yet,
didn't feel I had to, that afternoon in New York.
But when I consequently saw other films by Ozu
(which all confirmed the overwhelming first impression),
finally travelled to Tokyo (sic) for the first time
and for the only reason of seeing more of his work
that I could not find in Europe or America,
and when I eventually even made a film on his traces, *Tokyo-Ga*,
some of the mystery lifted.
No, that is not the right way to say it.
There *is* no mystery!
(And *that* is the lost secret, too!)

We are just not used any more to seeing a flow of images

where each and every one of them has nothing to hide,
shows nothing 'behind it',
instead means everything it shows us
and does not want or pretend to mean more.
We're used to automatically establishing some sort of ironic distance
between ourselves and whatever happens on the screen,
but in these films by Ozu
there is no need for any such irony or abstraction.
On the contrary:
they want us to let go of any predisposition, preconception or 'attitude'.

From a contemporary position
this might appear as a naive point of view,
both of the storyteller and of the stories told.
But I tend to believe the opposite:
our automatic distance,
our ironic (or cynical) stepping away from every 'film reality'
as something we have to keep ourselves out of
(in order to maintain our sanity),
is probably nothing but a defence mechanism.
If that reaction did not kick into action automatically,
we'd be extremely vulnerable.
Like children again ...

As children we definitely *did* function like this:
what we saw was what we accepted as given,
and what we received was also what we felt.
We didn't need any 'translation',
we were with all the people and all the things
and they were with us ...

It is certainly no coincidence
that children play an important part in Ozu's films,
only to mention one of his first 'talkies',
There was a Father, but ...
His children are in a world of their own,
only that their realm doesn't have all these rules
and makes much more sense.
Back to us: if we dare to let down that defence shield,
in the case of Ozu nothing will hurt us.
Nothing could be further remote from his universe
than afflicting any shock, or pain, or unease.

enduring images

I have to go into detail to explain this.
Ozu takes all the obstacles away
between his 'language'
and our own reception of it.

For instance:
the same lens for each and every shot, his
famous 50mm.
A quick explanation for all of you
who are not familiar with focal lengths and other optical issues:
our human vision corresponds to about a 35 or 38mm lens
in the classic realm of cinema which was entirely based on 35mm film.
That corresponds as much as possible to how we perceive the world.
A 28mm lens, or under, would already show the world slightly distorted,
in a 'wide angle',
which stretches space and makes things look more distanced.
A 50mm lens, however, already contracts space a bit.
From here on we go into a 'tele angle'.
Seen through a 50mm lens things appear just a tiny bit closer.
Not much, just ever so little.

So, Ozu's only lens condensed space slightly, almost imperceptibly.
You have less distance from things.
The world, in a way, becomes more 'present',
you are a bit nearer to everything.
Unlike any other filmmaker,
Ozu used this one lens exclusively,
for wide shots as well as for close-ups.
You might not notice this as a normal film audience
(and again: this is very subtle),
but in the long run it has the most fundamental effect!
All of a sudden,
our own eyes and *his*
can adjust to one another's,
can slowly adopt the same vision,
can lose the fear of being surprised,
can relax,
can *trust*.
On top of that, Ozu always uses the same camera position.
All his shots are done from the eye level
of somebody sitting on a tatami floor.
This is a very defenceless, peaceful position.

You always see somebody standing in front of you slightly from below,
which increases a feeling of respect and modesty towards 'the other'.
And as this is always the same point of view,
again it eliminates any fear of surprise.
You can let your armour down...

And then Ozu does something highly unusual
when two people are talking to each other in any intimate conversation.
In order to understand his outstanding approach
you have to recall how a dialogue usually happens in movies.
Normally you see an 'establishing shot' of two people in their situation,
so you know where this dialogue takes place,
then you see a 'two shot' from the side,
or an 'over-shoulder shot' from behind,
and then you see 'close-ups'.
In these close-ups the camera concentrates on one actor,
and the other one continues to speak 'off-camera',
if he (or she) speaks at all.
On the set, the off-camera actor
is normally present next to the camera during the shooting,
in order to help and support the actor 'on-camera',
who this way could look his (or her) partner in the eye.

That technical description leads to what I want to make you aware of:
the actor in his (or her) close-up normally looks past the camera,
let's say slightly to the left of it.
With the cut to his or her counterpart,
the other actor, in the reverse angle,
would then look slightly to the right of the camera.
This way you have the illusion, as a viewer,
that the two of them look at each other.
The entire history of cinema
uses this approach to any dialogue or conversation.

The actors look at each other, that is the agreed convention,
and thereby *we*, the audience, are watching *them* having their dialogue.
The very architecture of film shots
gives us the position of the (invisible) witness,
puts us at a certain distance,
which allows us to look at the dialogue without having to 'participate'.
We stay 'outside', literally.

enduring images

Now, when Ozu stages any intimate dialogue,
he does something extremely unusual,
which, in spite of its apparent simplicity,
– again, this might be mistaken as naive –
is rather highly accomplished and complex!
You see the situation,
in an establishing shot from that low angle,
you often see the 'two-shot' from the side, too.
And then you see close-ups, but very different ones!
(You might not even be aware of this,
because Ozu does this ever so subtly!)
The actors do *not* look at each other!
They both look at the lens, or very close to it!
In the shooting process that means
that the off-camera actor sits *behind* the camera, not next to it,
so the on-camera actor looks 'through the camera', so to speak,
to his (or her) counterpart.

And that leads indeed to the most amazing difference!
As the spectator, you are no longer 'outside'.
The two actors *look at you*,
make you become (at least subconsciously)
part of their conversation.
You're no longer the invisible witness!
I need to say this with even more emphasis:
you, the viewer, become both parts,
you are even the air in between them,
you are participating, if you want it or not.
You are *involved* like never before!

So Ozu uses extremely simple yet efficient methods
to tear down our defences
and to let us become part of common humanity.
We are part of 'his family',
everyday people just like all of them,
turn into them just by watching.
In that lost paradise, remember,
watching was being.
Children still do nothing else all the time.
We are capable of that, of course,
but only too scared to do so,
most of the time.

Peace needs us to become children again, somehow,
otherwise we can never even smell what peace is
and immerse into it.
Ozu's films let us glimpse back
into that basic condition for perceiving peace.
His filmmaking vision might have been paradisiac, once,
seen from today it is now strictly a utopian world.

*

sacred journeys

Ozu's films are like ritual practices of a sacred order. His unique style of filmmaking, his architecture of scenes and his approach to characters gives rise to the sacred and its beauty. Through this sacredness we have the freedom to partake in his films; he shows us without hostility or violence the lives of the characters and their experience. The sacred, then, far from being transcendent or the otherworldly, is simply the *world as it is*. And through his highly accomplished technical means we experience the piety of the world and our sense of belonging to it, which demonstrates our shared and common humanity.

The sacred in his films comes close to what the Romanian anthropologist Mircea Eliade describes as the cosmology of the sacred:

> The world (that is, our world) is a universe within which the sacred has already manifested itself, in which, consequently, the break-through from plane to plane has become possible and repeatable. It is not difficult to see why the religious moment implies the cosmogonic moment. The sacred reveals absolute reality and at the same time makes orientation possible; hence it *founds the world* in the sense that it fixes the limits and establishes the order of the world.[13]

Sacredness manifests in Ozu's framing of the image, inspired by a basic principle of Zen art, *mu* or nothingness, the paradoxical fullness and emptiness of the scene. The *mu* character, as Schrader describes, is often used to refer to the spaces between 'branches of a flower arrangement; the emptiness is the integral part of the form'. He describes Ma Yuan, painter and originator of the 'one-corner style', as having this *mu* aesthetic: '[he] painted only one corner of the canvas, leaving the remainder of the canvas blank. The emptiness, however, was part of the painting and not just an unpainted background. The simple fishing boat placed in one corner gives meaning to the whole space.'[14]

This wholeness and emptiness is skilfully depicted in a moving sequence from *Tokyo Story*: we see from a great distance Tomi and Shukichi seated on a sea wall at Atami. They are framed at 'one corner' of the scene and surrounded by the vastness of the sea. This distant shot gives us literally a 'sea of loneliness' – they are outcasts. The scene is historically poignant. Since the Fifties and Sixties, the traditional structure of looking after the elderly had changed, it became more common for elderly parents to be left alone and stranded by their children.

In the next shot, we see the couple seated on the sea wall, but from behind. They do not look at each other, but are looking *together* at the sea. As Tomi and Shukichi look out together, their intimacy is made more real. We are with them in their desolation, they are not objects of our gaze, we share their experience. The beach sequence shows a compassion that is a necessity of peace. The nothingness, the vastness of space and framing of the couple is *everything*, just as the more distant shots give us a sense of their closeness. Today intimacy is most often shown by sexual encounters or through tight close-ups; neither technique necessarily captures the pathos of things, or provides anything new about human relationships.

In these scenes, Ozu's camera simply waits, it doesn't enter the drama, and it is not rushing to find a different angle or point of view. Through each and every camera angle, then, we get a sense of awe, in each set-up and in each frame we encounter the whole, or 'holy' as the etymology of the word suggests, since it is in the relationship between the distinct parts of the scene that we get a feel for what exists beyond words, what is lived, felt and experienced.

metaphysics of the unforgettable

In the last scenes of *Tokyo Story*, after the death of Tomi, Shukichi is alone. We do not see her death, it is 'sacrificed' in the economy and temporal structure of the film, but through carefully structured scenes the sadness that surrounds the transition between life and death are strongly realised.

In the last sequence of shots, the youngest daughter Kyoko is in a primary school classroom, moving from group to group. As we hear the whistle of a train, Kyoko moves to the window and looks at her watch. With the cut to the railroad below, we see a train coming in the distance. In that train, Noriko is looking out the window; the mountains of Onomichi are in the distance. Noriko looks at Tomi's watch, given to her by Shukichi. The camera stays with Noriko's sadness for a few moments.

The next scene is a long shot of the father sitting alone by the veranda, looking at the sea. He is not facing the camera, he is gazing away, as he is fanning himself, and we feel the summer heat. This shot gives us a sense of intimacy; the camera does not disturb the father, we are seated alongside him at this distance, yet this shot is effective in bringing us closer to him.

Ozu quietly makes visible the unseen aspects of grief and loss, the atmosphere that exists between the characters and ourselves. His portrayal of characters and cinematic techniques echo Martin Buber's *I–You* relations that we discussed in Chapter 2. For Buber, *I–You* relations arise in our meetings and encounters with others; these meetings can reveal things we otherwise might not see, they can effect a change in perception. For instance, the train whistle we hear in the last sequence invites the connection to the whole context of Tomi's death, to each of the characters portrayed: Noriko, Kyoko and Shukichi silently contemplate the loss of Tomi and we share in their connected grief.

Ozu's films characterise the sphere that arises between *I–You*. Buber writes:

> The relation to the *You* is direct. No system of ideas, no foreknowledge, and no fancy intervene between *I* and *You*. The memory itself is transformed, as it plunges out of its isolation into the unity of the whole. No aim, no lust, and no anticipation intervene between *I* and *You*. Desire itself is transformed as it plunges out of its dream into the appearance. Every means is an obstacle. Only when every means has collapsed does the meeting come about.[15]

In Ozu's films, it is the quiet and still moments that give us space to think and feel. Ultimately, stillness heals. In *Tokyo Story* the cities of Onomichi and Tokyo themselves are the moments of transition and repose, the still shots of sea, factory chimneys, mountain views or hanging laundry give us the essential *mu* aesthetic, the space between stillness and action. Ozu's visual motifs are transitional moments that give us a state of repose that is essential for the characters, as much as it is for the viewer. In this space, we come close to the sacred and the holy in cinema.

In the very last sequence of *Tokyo Story* we share the stillness and sacred qualities of the everyday and its rhythms:

> 171. *The Hirayama house. Shukichi sits by the veranda and looks at the sea. Today again the woman next door speaks to him through the window.*
> **Woman:** Everyone's gone now? You'll be lonely, then.
> **Shukichi:** Well.
> **Woman:** It was really so sudden.

Father by Veranda
(from *Tokyo Story*, 1953)

Shukichi: Oh, she was a headstrong woman ... but if I knew things would come to this, I'd have been kinder to her. (*The woman says nothing.*) Living alone like this, days will be long.
Woman: You will be lonely.
She leaves. By himself, Shukichi looks out over the sea. A long silence.
172. *The sea. A small island boat goes by.*
173. *Shukichi by the veranda looking vaguely out over the sea.*
174. *The ocean. The sound of the boat becomes as a distant dream. It is a July afternoon in the Inland sea.*[16]

*

Peace manifests in the sacred. What we experience in Ozu's films is the awesome quality of everyday life, as well as a unique sense of belonging. His films invite a model for an ethical life, they demonstrate how to act toward each other with benevolence and kindness. What we learn from Ozu is that in the *no-thingness* of universal experience, everything becomes possible.

The following are excerpts from Ozu's diaries. The diary entries date from 1960, when Ozu was shooting *Late Autumn*.

Friday, the 9th (of September)
It rained, but it didn't last long. 'The small apartment' with Hara (Setsuko) and Tsukasa (Yôko): fifth day. Chûjô Sachiko came to the shoot. She brought me a shirt from 'Sibata's'. The rain stopped in the early afternoon. We finished in time. Went looking at the set for the inn. In the evening the sky was entirely clear again. 'Autumn sky in Bejing', by Uméhara Ryûzaburô. [A favourite painter of Ozu's.] Took a bath when I came home.

Saturday, the 10th
Sun. 'The small apartment' with Hara and Tsukasa : sixth day. We stayed inside the schedule, but somehow I didn't get it right. Even though it was Saturday, I called a cab and went home right away. A bath and saké. Sugimura Haruko sent me a card to thank me for the rolls of fabric. Went to bed early.

Note
   Woke up in the middle of the night, reread the script. Lots of errors jumped to my eyes. Is it because of the real difficulty of the work, or a hereditary laziness facing a difficulty? Watch out, not to betray your first decisions is of utmost importance!

Sunday, the 11th
   Clouds. Day of rest today. Sluggish morning. Bath, saké, siesta: here I am with the same habits as 'Shôsuké' (fairy-tale figure who spent all his time drinking and sleeping). Opening of the autumn sumo tournament. Three 'Ozekis' and one 'Yokuzuna' were beaten today. Again saké and a bath, before drawing my storyboard…

Monday, the 12th
   Clouds. Studio. With Hara and Tsukasa in the morning. With Hara and Okada (Mariko) in the afternoon. It started to rain. Sada received a 'hanten' (traditional workman's kimono) from Toshinishiki. Rain. End of the Olympic Games in Rome.

Tuesday, the 13th
   Clouds. 'The small apartment': eighth day of shooting. Hara, Tsukasa at Okada in the morning and afternoon. A bit of rain. Saw the rushes. Went to bed early, and woke up at midnight. Couldn't find rest until three. Storyboard.

Wednesday, the 14th
   Clouds, then clear sky. 'The small apartment': ninth day. Last scene with Hara and Okada. It was bad and I preferred to stop it. Lunch break, then sound recording at the KR studio on schedule. Kidney pains. Went home right away and went to bed.

[…]

Monday, the 31st October
   Rain, then sun. We gave up shooting because of the rain, which eventually stopped. Yoshizawa came. Played golf with Ryu and Hamada at Umégô. Siesta. In the evening I went to the library. Visit by Yoshishigé; he told us about the United States, and showed us

some 8mm film. The crew went by bus to the Maoka Inn of Mr Tajiri. Second night at the 'Yamafuji'.

Tuesday, the 1st of November
We left before 8 for the shoot at the Noda golf course. Tentative sun. The end of shooting has finally come. With me were Ryû (Chishu) , Hamada and Nobuzô (Nakamura). Return by taxi. From 16:00h on, viewing rushes at the studio with the director and Tsukimori. At home: bath and saké. Am tired. Last day before the full moon....

[...]

Saturday, the 31st of December
Clouds. Murakami went back and left by cab during the day. Bacon, 'Zôsui' with chicken, miso soup and 'Hamachi' fish. Siesta. Glacial temperature. I put drops into my eyes ... Got a bit drunk on saké. Thirty-five years of a career: thirty-five years of slow retirement!

Memo
>At the side of the road,
>the stone Buddha
>is covered with snow,
>indifferent to time
>and all preoccupation.
>
>When I drink saké
>I enter a world
>where, 'abracadabra',
>time consumes itself
>like wood in a fireplace.[17]

Policeman in the Field, Heiligendamm, Germany, 2007
(Wim Wenders)

War and Eros are the two sources of illusion and falsehood among men. Their mixture represents the very greatest impurity.
Simone Weil

4

Imagining the Real

Peace requires imagination. To invent peace is to imagine the real, and this imagination requires the consideration of how war has so thoroughly captured our cultures, as well as how to create an alternative response to it. War has a hold on our cultural imaginations as an inevitable force, it is peace that has no benefactor. Unless we imagine peace in its light along with its 'darkness', it is difficult to imagine alternative responses to violence. The transcendental and sacred qualities of peace are not otherworldly, but lived and experienced.

To imagine peace – and its worldly qualities – involves a renewal of stories, values and beliefs. In some instances, it is images that 'shock' us out of habitual ways of looking that can offer the alternative visions of hope and peace. As previously discussed, this involves a creative 'revolt' to change perceptual habits rather than continuing historical trauma and grief (see Chapter 2). In this chapter, we look at the imagination required to transform images of violence and war, not by reproducing them, but rather how through a lens of compassion, humility and grace we can imagine and reinvent them. This imagination can lead to a re-enchantment with the world and our usual ways of looking at it.[1]

grand illusions

Necessarily peace is altogether different from the logic of war, but we have a 'terrible love of war', as James Hillman writes.[2] Much of human history shows that violence is deeply embedded in the structures of our cultural imaginations and morality. In this way, grief and loss cannot be transformed when war and its vicissitudes have a hold on the human psyche and conscience. With such a diabolical hold on our imaginations, it is often difficult for reparation to take place and to find solace. In this light, how we understand justice and the 'good' as well as the 'forces of evil' can be misguided.

In 1938, Anglo-American poet W.H. Auden wrote a most exquisite poem on the legacies of war and cultural belief entitled 'Here war is simple like a monument':

> Here war is simple like a monument:
> A telephone is speaking to a man;
> Flags on a map assert that troops were sent;
> A boy brings milk in bowls. There is a plan
>
> For living men in terror of their lives,
> Who thirst at nine who were to thirst at noon,
> And can be lost and are, and miss their wives,
> And, unlike an idea, can die too soon.
>
> But ideas can be true although men die,
> And we can watch a thousand faces
> Made active by one lie:
>
> And maps can really point to places
> Where life is evil now:
> Nanking; Dachau.[3]

Auden's poem establishes a moment of reflection in amongst the horrors of war; his poem brings us closer to the language of the wounded (as John Berger asks: 'Who, still on the battlefield, wants monuments?').[4] War establishes monuments in its wake just as it establishes cultural values and beliefs, yet it is remembrance of a different order that gives words to the suffering and wounded. When war is understood as a system of contract and is seen as inevitable it instils a language of courage, heroism and loyalty for all. Loyalty, unity and belonging in this sense are based on separation and on the division of time and space. Rather than belonging together, we are divided into categories of people – *us* and *them* – as well as the moral frames of good versus evil. Berger notes the opposite of love is not hate, but separation.[5]

French filmmaker Jean Renoir's 1937 anti-war film, *La Grande illusion*, captures this illusion with the following scene: the two main film protagonists and prisoners of war Maréchal and Rosenthal, pursued by the German army, arrive at an open field surrounded by mountains, and what they encounter is the ultimate 'grand illusion':

Maréchal: Are you sure that's Switzerland?
Rosenthal: I'm sure.
Maréchal: They're so alike.
Rosenthal: Of course, frontiers were invented by men not by Nature.

*

'Erect no monument', Rilke declares in his *Sonnets to Orpheus*, first published in 1923.[6] Rilke's sonnets portray a love for others, songs of grace and tenderness.[7] How do we create these 'songs of peace', different virtues of love and heroism, as well as humility and grace? Generally speaking, it is through the creation of myths and stories that intangible elements of cultures can be communicated as well as provide a certain sense of morality and ethics – our ethical imaginations.[8] As Emmanuel Levinas says elsewhere, it is not just ethics alone that generates this quest, but the pursuit of the 'holy, the holiness of the holy'.[9] This 'holy' quest is about 'the time of others' – an almost primordial responsibility – that demands us to respond to the radical uniqueness and presence of others in this world, and beyond our usual frontiers of understanding.[10] This is the terrain of justice and the good.

Today, when the media announce nothing but violence, they are providing no detail whatsoever,[11] no time for reflection, imagination or solace. The result is the dislocation of time and how we understand our sense of identity and place. Mircea Eliade has noted that previous cosmological explanations of the world as well as mythical stories incorporated the time of living and the time of creation as the necessary conditions of life – a sacred time.[12] There was a direct and unmediated experience to place; dwelling was part of a cosmic union as well as the cultivation of belonging and community.

Essentially, we need to take a fresh look at sacred ideas, rites and symbols that can rejuvenate cultural myths and stories by imagining the real without fear or violence. Even more so, there is a need to explore the awesome qualities of the sacred, since the sacred – as we discussed in previous chapters – can evoke terror as well as beauty; it is often the terrible and the fearful that have the most powerful force over us and dictate how we understand cultural rites and rituals. At a deeper level, then, our desires and yearnings become the strange fusion of terror and awe, when the sacred becomes the 'illusion' of truth and truth the demarcation of separation (what French anthropologist René Girard might call in his language 'monstrous doubles').[13]

Eliade reminds us that the sacred is saturated with being, it has power; sacred power in this sense 'means reality and at the same time enduringness and efficacity'. Put differently, the sacred is a deep desire 'to *be*, to participate in *reality*, to be saturated with power'.[14] How the sacred is understood in our cultures, its social reality, gives rise to the power to create or to destroy; it can provide both a sense of belonging and connection to the world and its potency, or just as well a sense of detachment and alienation. Let us take a look at the awesome qualities of the sacred and myth-making that can inspire the words and images for peace, and its ethical means.

a poem of force

French philosopher and social activist Simone Weil's essay 'The *Iliad* or the Poem of Force', published on the eve of World War Two, is a reflection on Homer's epic poem as well as a reflection on the looming world war. In Weil's account, Homer's mythic tale is a pacifist story par excellence, as she argues that most Greek myths and legends are steeped in war, but the futility of such force is laid bare in this poem. For her, the true subject of the *Iliad* is force; force makes a human into a 'thing', enslaving everyone, who must at some point bow their neck to its power – masters and slaves alike:

> In this work, at all times, the human spirit is shown as modified by its relations with force, as swept away, blinded, by the very force it imagined it could handle, as deformed by the weight of the force it submits to. For those dreamers who considered that force, thanks to progress, would soon be a thing of the past, the *Iliad* could appear as historical document; for others, whose powers of recognition are more acute and perceive force, today as yesterday, at the very centre of human history, the *Iliad* is the purest and loveliest of mirrors.[15]

Glories of war are short lived in the *Iliad*, as force changes sides like a seesaw. Violence is habitually repeated in the name of what is considered to be just in the light of the gods and in their human incarnations. Long before the Gospels, Weil writes, the *Iliad* gives a sense of how violence is recreated through a sacrificial tone in almost the same terms. She states:

> By its very blindness, destiny establishes a kind of justice. Blind also is she who decrees to warriors punishment in kind. He that takes the sword, will perish by the sword ...
> 'Ares is just, and kills those who kill.'[16]

Throughout human history there are very few mythic tales and heroic figures that show the generosity to abdicate power and force, to provide an alternative to violence.
Weil notes:

> To respect life in somebody else when you have had to castrate yourself of all yearning for it demands a truly heartbreaking exertion of the powers of generosity. It is impossible to imagine any of Homer's warriors being capable of such an exertion, unless it is that warrior who dwells, in a peculiar way, at the very center of the poem – I mean Patroclus, who 'knew how to be sweet to everybody', and throughout

the *Iliad* commits no cruel or brutal act. But then how many men do we know, in several thousand of years of human history, who would have displayed such god-like generosity? Two or three? – even this is doubtful. Lacking this generosity, the conquering soldier is like a scourge of nature. Possessed by war, he, like the slave, becomes a thing, though his manner of doing so is different – over him too, words are powerless as over matter itself. And both, at the touch of force, experience its inevitable effects: they become deaf and dumb. Such is the nature of force.[17]

What the *Iliad* suggests is that we do not step into a universe from the outside; we are already in it, we live in a time of force, and in this very time we must learn, as Weil writes:

... there is no refuge from fate, learn not to admire force, not to hate the enemy, nor to scorn the unfortunate. How soon this will happen is another question.[18]

Whether we use force creatively or destructively becomes a matter of choice to be invented, but humans confuse the power of force and its creative and destructive tendencies. To understand the terrible love of force requires imagination – that is, the creative means to respond to this love of force with compassion and mercy.

chaos

Japanese director Akira Kurosawa's 1985 film *Ran* retells the story of Shakespeare's *King Lear*. Through the retelling of this Shakespearean tragedy and its deep cultural legacy, Kurosawa demonstrates the futility of force and violence through benevolence, compassion and piety. In the following, we specifically focus on *Ran* to draw attention to the conditions required for peace and the potential for forgiveness, grace and humility.

In Shakespeare's *Lear*, King Lear divides his land among his three daughters, the two eldest daughters flatter Lear and the youngest speaks the truth. The story is of loyalty and truthfulness, and of the struggle over land and territory. The most faithful daughter, Cordelia, in her devotion and loyalty to Lear himself is condemned to death, breaking Lear's heart. In Kurosawa's film, the story is set in sixteenth-century Japan, where an ageing ruler, Lord Hidetora, divides his land between his sons. In the same light as Lear, two elder sons bestow flattery upon him, the youngest when he speaks the truth is banished. In the film, Kurosawa does not flinch from demonstrating the violence of such struggles between family and its consequences.

Kurosawa's precision in filmmaking draws on Japanese spiritual art and craftsmanship. We saw this mastery through Ozu's work in exploring the intimacy of family life and conflict as well as cultural change. In Kurosawa, we see the epic versions of these struggles and their cultural legacy. Kurosawa's images are beautiful and sharp. He demonstrates injustice alongside the natural beauty of the world; the mountains and the sky are the arena in which human violence and force are played out, yet the world's beauty even in the theatre of war cannot be destroyed.

Kurosawa demonstrates the topography of what Girard calls 'violence and the sacred' in his book of the same name.[19] For Girard, the logic of violence is foundational to most cultural myths and stories. He argues that in most religious and spiritual practices there is a primordial connection between violence and the sacred. This connection is based on human desire – what he calls a 'mimetic' desire that makes us rivals not against the enemy, but against our own desires and kin relations. It is this internal rivalry or doubling effect that makes sacrifice necessary and casts out the 'enemy'. Girard maintains that many foundational stories of Western cultures such as the story of Cain and Abel see this rivalry and sacrifice through its moral consequences. He writes that this logic of violence essentially announces violence in such a way:

Now that I have killed my brother, everyone can kill me . . .[20]

In Kurosawa's *Ran*, the third son, Saburo, is banished as he makes the same type of observation to his father, Lord Hidetora:

Saburo: Even in a sheaf three arrows can be broken.
Hidetora: More of your pranks! Stop being foolish.
Saburo: It's you who are foolish. Your plan is absurd.
   You're either senile or mad.
Hidetora: Silence!
   Don't insult your father. What madness have I spoken?
   Wherein lies my senility?
Saburo: What kind of world do we live in?
   One barren of loyalty and feeling.
Hidetora: I'm aware of that!
Saburo: So you should be! You've spilled merciless blood. You showed
   no mercy, no pity.

> We too are children of this age, weaned on strife and chaos. We are your sons yet you count on our fidelity?
> In my eyes, that makes you a senile old fool!
> **Hidetora:** So that's it!
> You mean that one day you will forget I'm your father and betray me?
> **Saburo:** More folly.
> Does a traitor betray himself?
> **Hidetora:** Then you mean your brothers?
> **Saburo** (*turns to the second brother, Jiro*): He's jealous of Taro's position.
> **Jiro:** Is that why you slander me.
> Brother or not, watch yourself.
> **Saburo:** Your lesson of the three arrows was wasted.
> The unity of the three sons is split.

*

Kurosawa's *Ran* makes credible the violence in which everyone is caught, how the sacred is fused with the awesome force of doubles, of the fatal misunderstanding of loyalty and belonging – this is the thrust of a 'mimetic trap' that Girard speaks of. And it is through this strange fusion of desire and longing that human conflict is played out in a 'hall of mirrors'. What the film does, however, is demonstrate compassion and humility towards the characters in all of their vulnerability. By making the story credible, rather than 'showing' us the violence for violence's sake, we see how everyone 'bow[s] his neck to force', as Weil might put it, 'force is as pitiless to the man who possesses it, or thinks he does, as it is to its victims; the second it crushes, the first it intoxicates. The truth is, nobody really possesses it.'[21]

Kurosawa's work raises the question of how to deal with such a violent logic – that is, how to make a form of reparation possible. The violence in the film becomes a 'technical' problem rather than gratuitous violence. Kurosawa is not interested in glorifying violence but in demonstrating its effects. There is a difference between 'showing' violence and understanding the logic of violence. For instance, Italian filmmaker Pier Paolo Pasolini's 1975 film *Salò* 'shows' violence, but doesn't necessarily transform it. Certainly, *Salò* gives the viewer a sense of the perverse desire and power attached to fascism and violence, but it often leaves viewers stuck in the trauma, so to speak.[22] Whereas exploring violence through a more compassionate lens can demonstrate how desire, power and violence co-exist in our cultures, and how to understand and transform them creatively.

forgiveness

Each of the characters in *Ran* has the threat of force and destruction looming, and it is in this light that the benevolence of the film demonstrates the sorrow and mourning that are tied together in the landscape of violence. Through the character of Lady Sué, the wife of the second brother, there is a link to fundamental sorrow and pity that is part of non-violence. We can feel this sorrow in the following scene where Hidetora confronts Lady Sué:

> *Lady Sué is singing: Praise be to Buddha.*
> **Hidetora:** I knew you'd be here.
> **Lady Sué:** Father-in-law!
> **Hidetora:** Never mind the ceremony. It's been a long time. Let me look at you.
> Still the same sad face. When I see you, it breaks my heart. It's worse when you smile.
> I burned down your castle. Your father and mother perished. And you look at me like that.
> Look upon me with hatred. It would be easier to bear.
> Go on, hate me!
> **Lady Sué:** I don't hate you.
> All is decided in our previous lives. The Buddha embraces all things.
> **Hidetora:** Buddha again!
> He is gone from this evil world.
> His guardians are in exile.
> You can't rely on Buddha's mercy.

In another scene, Lady Sué's brother Tsurumaru, blinded by Hidetora as a young boy, comes across Hidetora when he arrives mad and unexpected at his door. He responds to Hidetora through the 'music of the heart' and sorrow, rather than retaliation. What Tsurumaru demonstrates is a genuine hospitality that embraces the suffering as well as vulnerability of others, including Hidetora. Forgiveness is offered through a different means, as memory and violence of the past is not forgotten, but Tsurumaru's character invites us to move *toward* the past with a certain grace and acceptance.

> **Hidetora:** Tsurumaru!
> **Tsurumaru:** It's been a long time ... Lord Hidetora.
> **Hidetora:** You remember me?
> **Tsurumaru:** How could I forget you?
> I was only a boy, but could I forget the man who burned down our castle? Who in exchange for my life gouged out my eyes?

> I try to be like my sister, to pray to the Buddha and rid myself of hatred. But not one day do I forget!
> Not one night do I sleep in peace!
> I regret I cannot welcome you as befits the Great Lord. Luckily, my sister gave me a flute.
> I will play for you.
> Anything else, I give you hospitality of the heart. It is the only pleasure left to me.
> *Tsurumaru begins playing his flute.*

Sorrow is akin to the word 'sorry'; sorrow in its aesthetic and moral feeling may open the space of forgiveness. When we open ourselves to be *with* others, with their sorrow and grief, forgiveness may become possible. Although it may not always lead to immediate reconciliation and justice, it opens the way toward it.

*

Kurosawa recounts in his autobiography the aftermath of the Great Kanto Earthquake of 1923: the Sumidagawa River filled with corpses, blood and bodies not only from the quake, but also from the massacre of Koreans, who were blamed for the quake (Chris Marker's 1985 documentary film *AK* cites this example as gross human stupidity).[23] In Kurosawa's words, he and his elder brother, who were both children at the time, saw the bodies, and as much as Kurosawa wanted to turn away, his brother told him to 'look carefully now'. He believed the sight would plague him with nightmares, since the horror was unbearable, but Kurosawa writes that he did not have nightmares from the horror. Asking his brother how this could be so, his brother answered:

> 'If you shut your eyes to a frightening sight, you end up being frightened. If you look at everything straight on, there is nothing to be afraid of.' Looking back on that excursion now, I realize it must have been horrifying for my brother too. It had been an expedition to conquer fear.[24]

To look carefully is a requirement for peace. Kurosawa sees. His films offer a modern incarnation of sorrow and grief, as well as the perplexities of human violence, with compassion rather than gratuity. We are reminded that the human soul has potential for compassion and forgiveness even in a state of turmoil. The choice is ours.

end of violence?

I made the film *The End of Violence* quite spontaneously.
I had come back to Los Angeles in 1996 after a long absence
(having lived there for seven years in the Eighties)
and was struck by an increase in paranoia.
There were signs on every front yard
that intruders had to face an 'armed response',
there were security cameras everywhere,
and even a very sweet elderly lady who had once been my neighbour
now slept with a gun under her pillow
and kept it with her in a plastic bag on the way to the supermarket.

I realised that the city, in an almost absurd way,
was suffering from the backlash of one of its own main export articles:
violence.
Violence had become an ingredient of almost any film,
whether its story needed it or not.
At some point earlier on, in the Sixties and Seventies,
if I remember correctly,
'sex' had been such a popular 'all-over ingredient' for movies,
but sex was out now, violence was in.

Zapping through American television channels
was an instant proof of
its omnipresence,
and it seemed that in movies, too,
the level of acceptance of physical and psychological violence
had been raised enormously.

People were scared of attacks,
of the latent possibility that their houses or cars were invaded.
Hijacking cars had become a common thing,
so you would only drive with your doors locked from inside,
and luxury cars were all equipped with devices
firmly installed in a place where they could not be reached easily
that would transmit signals so you could trace them everywhere.
Hijacked cars could be located from the air by helicopters
and chased down minutes after they were seized.

The omnipresence of fear as well as of surveillance
became the instant subject of a film I then quickly wrote
together with my screenwriter, Nicholas Klein.
The lead character is a film producer by the name of Mike Max...
He has built his fortune on violence-driven movies,
when he all of a sudden becomes the subject of a vicious attack on his life.
He barely escapes and then tries to figure out
who could possibly be after him.
In order to 'disappear' he becomes a gardener,
a member of the army of Mexican or Hispanic helpers
who keep the city running.
He can now even observe his own house, undetected;
as a Mexican he has practically become invisible.

He soon finds out that he is linked to a bigger plot,
in which 'surveillance' plays the key part.
For that, we conceived the total reversal of cause and effect.
A security system is installed by a secret service agency
that watches over the city from satellites,
and from a myriad of cameras planted everywhere.
The headquarters are at the Observatory.
It had once been used to watch space from the Earth,
now it is used to watch Earth from space.

And the security cameras are not only installed to observe,
but are also linked to devices
that enable them to actually and literary 'shoot'.
The common synonym for 'taking pictures' as 'shooting pictures'
is for once taken seriously.

It all made a lot of sense, I figured,
even if there was a science-fiction element to the whole thing.
The machinery to prevent violence
certainly has the propensity to cause it, or increase it.

*

humility

In Robert Bresson's 1966 film *Au hasard Balthazar* the main character, Balthazar, the donkey, gives us an alternative model to violence and its pervasiveness in our cultures. His character offers ways to reconsider the circuit of violence and its human production. Through the donkey's eyes we see human cruelty and exploitative means, just as the donkey is enslaved by the violence that surrounds him, but he does not reproduce it. The donkey observes human life without judgement (we must remember, too, a donkey's view of the world is sideways). In some ways, Balthazar's story echoes Christ's humility and his serving of others. At the last supper, Christ washes his disciples' feet with respect, care and dignity even in the light of betrayal and violence. It is this story that opens the way for considering a non-sacrificial approach to violence.

As Girard writes, there is another logic far superior to violence that recognises violence and sacrifice but does not take part in it – this 'non-violence' demonstrates the force of violence, but with humility and 'hospitality for the truth'.[25] Girard suggests this is the story of Christ and his crucifixion. He argues that the story understood as *non-sacrificial* opens the way for a different relation to the sacred. He writes of the Gospels:

> There must be no hesitation about giving one's own life in order not to kill, so as to break out, by this action, from the circle of murder and death. It is quite literally true, when we are concerned with the confrontation of *doubles*, that he who wishes to save his life will lose it; he will be obliged, in effect, to kill his brother, and that means dying in a state of fatal misunderstanding of the other and of himself. He who agrees to lose his life will keep it for eternal life, for he alone is not a killer, he alone knows the fullness of love.[26]

It is this love that has yet to be fully understood in modern myths and stories.

In *Au hasard Balthazar*, the donkey's humility reflects in some ways the non-violent and non-sacrificial elements of Girard's point on violence and the sacred. It is the sacrificial need to *kill* others that emerges in an economy of violence and that designates what becomes sacred or disavowed in cultures. The film certainly displays violence and sacrifice, but through the donkey's observations it brings together a different spiritual unity and logic.

In one of the saddest and most poignant moments of the film, the donkey is shot at a border crossing, surrounded by a herd of sheep. He eventually dies alone in an open pasture. He dies without retribution or retaliation; it is this death without retaliation that Girard speaks of when he recognises there is a logic that moves beyond violence. The donkey is a spiritual reminder of humility and grace, he observes violence, but in his humility he does not partake in it. Through the donkey's observations we see the human capacity for evil more precisely, more clearly, and in this clarity we are asked to consider the implications of the violence that surrounds him, and the choices made by others.

The death of Balthazar in the film has a weight unlike human violence, because the donkey has no language that can express grief; surrounded by lambs in his death, the images of the film evoke a spiritual unity between the animal and his environment, while shedding light on moral and human blindness. One of the last lines of the film declares Balthazar as a saint; what makes him saintly is his acceptance of others, even if it is painful for 'us' to see the violence of others and its effects.

seeing through the eyes of a donkey

Mary and I watched Au hasard Balthazar together,
– for me it was about forty years after I first saw it –
and the film so much troubled me,
that I watched it two more times afterwards, with different people.
I was still deeply disturbed.
How could an 'old film' from the Sixties
be so utterly violent and unsettling?

For the longest time you watch this movie thinking
that you're looking at the story of a donkey named Balthazar,
and that his fate is told through the eyes of all these people
who cross his life.
The film starts very innocently.
Balthazar is very cute when he is young
(like all baby animals),
and then he gets grittier and uglier.
He is beaten and pushed around,
and he carries any load patiently.
He can only utter his pain and misery with his plaintive brays.
We get to know the people in Balthazar's life.
His first owner, a girl and soon a reclusive young woman, Marie,
who gives the donkey its name,
her parents, especially her stubborn schoolmaster of a father,
a bad boy, Gérard, whom Marie later falls in love with,

a tramp, Arnold, who owns Balthazar for a while
and a rich man who exploits him mercilessly.

So we're thinking we watch the life of a donkey
from the point of view of all the people who determine his fate,
see the poor creature suffer,
while he in turn sees the poor people around him suffer,
and that's that.
After all, he's a donkey, and we are people.
We have our sympathies for some of the characters,
and despise some of the others.
And we definitely have empathy for Balthazar.

Until we suddenly realise:
the whole thing has really turned the other way around!
An astonishing reversal has happened,
and it is hard to say, *when* it really occurred:
we're no longer on the safe territory
of watching a donkey's story through the eyes of people – no,
we're watching our fellow humans through the eyes of a donkey!

Balthazar is the witness (sometimes the only one)
of the fates of all these characters that determine his life.
As he watches their lives go down the drain
and all of them become victims of each other,
the point of view of the donkey becomes more and more dominant,
until we have somehow totally identified with him, the creature.

And the most amazing thing is happening now:
it is the humans that become 'creatures'.
Arnold the beggar dies miserably,
driven to his death by the local tough guys
falling drunkenly off Balthazar's back
(nobody else to stand by him during his last moments),
Marie's father dies, catatonic, without a word,
even refusing the help of the priest,
but most of all Marie is ending like a caged animal,
crouched into a corner of the room,
naked, beaten, abandoned.
In comparison to these endings of our human heroes,
Balthazar passes away in an almost heavenly way.
He is surrounded by sheep,

who accompany him gently to his death.
And Balthazar dies
with the most gentle and content expression on his face;
yes, by now it has become a face, indeed,
his eyes have turned from the eyes of a 'beast of burden'
to the eyes of a saint,
full of wisdom and understanding.

'Creature sees man' ...
Now this is not just a small or discreet shift of the point of view.
This is radical.
When have you ever seen the world through the eyes of an animal?!
The most disturbing and shocking thing is:
the eyes of the creature are more gentle than the eyes of man.

In any film we tend to adopt the point of view of the hero,
even if the hero is a bad guy(!) by sheer identification.
Films do that.
They force us to interiorise the film's 'viewing architecture':
there is a face and eyes that look,
and with the next cut we see what these eyes see
and already, subconsciously, we assume the p.o.v. of that person.
Even against our will we start seeing with his (or her) eyes.
We *become* that person, that character,
because the film forces his (or her) look on us.
In Bresson's film we become a donkey!
The film shows us the long sad face of Balthazar,
and more and more Bresson cuts to what he sees,
and if we want it or not, we are hooked.
In the end, *we are Balthazar*.

Seeing through someone else's eyes is certainly a very important lesson,
or call it a 'tool of perception',
in any confrontation or dialogue,
but especially in any peace process.
To be open to a different point of view, literally,
and thereby allow yourself to adopt another person's perspective,
understand the thinking, the suffering, the pain or satisfaction,
shortly: the very existence of another being,
isn't that the nature of the I–YOU relationship
that according to Martin Buber makes us who we are?

Bresson takes that lesson very far.
At one point in the story, the donkey gets a job in a zoo
and is used to deliver straw for the caged animals.
Balthazar looks at the lion,
and the lion looks at him.
Balthazar looks at the polar bear,
and the polar bear looks at him.
Balthazar looks at the elephant
and the elephant looks at him.
The animals look at each other, eye to eye,
mysteriously connected,
and mysteriously freed from human interference.
We watch them communicate without us.
Their silent conversations do in fact exclude us.
A song by David Byrne comes to my mind.

> They like to laugh at people
> They're setting a bad example
> They have untroubled lives
> They think everything's nice
>
> They're thinking they know what's best
> They're making a fool of us ...

We almost hear the animals' voices in that silent dialogue,
even if we have to make them up in our minds.
They speak of suffering, of exploitation,
or resignation and of the distant longing for freedom.
Eye to eye, there is sheer empathy, understanding, and peace.
Like in our human realm, too
(I'm tempted to add 'originally'),
whenever we're facing each other person to person.

What is it that has driven that empathy out of our existences
(at least as it is in the case of the cast of characters in Bresson's film)
and made us incapable to share each other's point of view?
That is the cruel question we're exposed to
watching *Au hasard Balthazar* even forty years later.
What is it in the human condition
that tries to impose our own view onto others,
without the ability, capacity, propensity,
to receive somebody else's openly?

imagining the real 123

Balthazar Surrounded by the Sheep
(from *Au hasard Balthazar*, 1966)

*

hope

How do we receive others openly? How can we respond to violent events without reproducing them? Pablo Picasso's 1937 painting *Guernica* portrays an artistic response to suffering and violence; he offers something uniquely human in the midst of the despair and tragedy of war. Picasso's rapid response and fury to the air-raid bombing of the Basque village of Guernica in Spain makes the terror of the event credible to the imagination through its visual imagery, just as it depicts a violence that is unthinkable at a cultural level. Historically speaking, this was one of the first aerial bombings to target a civilian population. In many ways, the painting questions archetypes of memory and culture through its disturbing imagery and the horrors of the event.

Picasso reassembles the world where myth and real come together and are torn apart: animals, humans, birds, buildings are dislocated and fragmented. The painting has an almost cinematic quality and presence; time and space are momentarily suspended, as everything is shattered – not only the physical world, but also the soul of the world. Through his use of black and white, the intensity and shades of black, white and grey, he paints the story of fallen bodies and this shattered world. The matter and memory of this exploded world calls us forth and asks us to look, but in a different way.

Buried among the carnage in the painting is the outline of a dove, blackened by the paint, cut by a dagger-like strip of white paint. The dove is the last vestige of hope, but how do we understand this fallen dove? Since biblical times, the dove has occupied the role as the teller of good fortune and the hope for humanity. It is its peaceful symbol and myth, the holy spirit incarnate, winged, stimulating, inspiring. The presence and holiness of the white dove is indeed the archetype of 'spirit'.

Picasso's dove is broken, it is blacked out and screaming. How do we repair this rupture, this break? What do we do with this screaming composite of a dove? T.S. Eliot offers his incarnation of the dove that emulates World War Two dive-bombers:

Guernica
(Pablo Picasso, 1937 © Succession Picasso/DACS, London)

> The dove descending breaks the air
> With flame of incandescent terror
> Of which the tongues declare
> The one discharge from sin and error.
> The only hope, or else despair
>   Lies in the choice of pyre or pyre –
>   To be redeemed from fire by fire.
> Who then devised the torment? Love.
> Love is the unfamiliar Name
> Behind the hands that wove
> The intolerable shirt of flame
> Which human power cannot remove.
>   We only live, only suspire
>   Consumed by either fire or fire.[27]

Picasso's screaming dove and Eliot's dove provide an alternative response to the awesome but terrible events of war. Paradoxical as it may seem, Picasso and Eliot point us toward the necessity of peace because we can imagine the horrors of war, but through different means. Picasso's *Guernica* allows us to *look* at a moment in time and observe it by standing still, just as he as the painter has to observe a moment carefully with his artistic sensibility and sight. In Eliot's poetry, we experience the sacred in the light of horror through the rhythm of his language and its stillness. In each case, the artists 'create what they see', they transform the relations of the real and the imaginary. And through their creative dialogue with unthinkable events there is the possibility of transforming perception. There is a way of seeing that can respond to violence without reproducing the trauma and paralysing others and ourselves.

Picasso's and Eliot's creative works and poetic force give something uniquely human in the midst of the violence: the quality of being able to *hold still* long enough to suggest a response that transforms how we see the event. While both responses deal with civilian death, they do not ask for retribution, only for another form of hope and courage, a time and place *for* peace.

As Eliot writes elsewhere in the *Four Quartets*:

> I said to my soul, be still, and wait without hope
> For hope would be hope for the wrong thing; wait without love
> For love would be love of the wrong thing; there is yet faith
> But the faith and the love and hope are all in the waiting.
> Wait without thought, for you are not ready for thought:
> So the darkness shall be the light, and the stillness the dancing.[28]

grace

Danish film director Carl Theodor Dreyer's films evoke grace and mercy. All of Dreyer's films in one way or another deal with the unknown qualities and spiritual dimensions of everyday life, but also how religious dogma and its incarnations can paralyse people and communities. For instance, in Dreyer's 1955 film *Ordet* (The Word), based on a play by Kaj Munk, there is a striking concentration of beauty and grace as well as the effects of religious fundamentalism. The film is based on two opposing families, a tailor's poor family and a rich farming family. Each, in their own way, has strong religious beliefs, and a long history of antagonism toward each other. Alongside the rigidity of the characters – against the harshness and cruelty of human belief systems – we see the potential for generosity and tolerance, a *suffering together* with others, not superiority over others.

Dreyer believed that our cultures have too narrow a definition of realism and mysticism. For him, it is the role of cinema as artistic expression to alter this reality, to create a new kind of 'realism'. In such a way, it is through Dreyer's cinematic architecture that we observe the cruelty and human violence with a certain mercy. His films give a sense of quietude, a harmonious style and rhythm in which to observe conflict. How does he do this? Reflecting on his film *Day of Wrath*, a film that is about the religious persecution of women, Dreyer considers how the 'eye' looks, and he composes the images in a more harmonious way.[29] Developing his own aesthetic 'realism', Dreyer maintains that the eye prefers a 'certain order' and harmony in movement. He writes:

> The eye prefers order, and therefore it is of importance that the picture effects are harmonious and remain so even in movement. Ungraceful lines push the spectator's eye.
>
> The eye absorbs horizontal lines rapidly and easily repels vertical lines. The eye is involuntarily attracted by objects in motion but remains passive over stationary things. This is the explanation why the eye, with pleasure, follows gliding camera movements, preferably when they are soft and rhythmic. As a principle rule, one can say that one shall try to keep a continuous, flowing, horizontally gliding motion in the film. If one then suddenly introduces vertical lines, one can reach an instantly dramatic effect – as, for instance, in the pictures of the vertical ladder just before it is thrown into the fire in *Day of Wrath*.[30]

Dreyer's films often involve long takes and almost static scenes. In this way, his films are similar to paintings. Dreyer asks us to look, and to look slowly as events often unfold in real time. His cinematic images are carefully orchestrated. Each image makes us pause as we witness the story unfold. And through the distillation of images – there is nothing superfluous in Dreyer's images – everything has its place, and everything in its place is exacting and precise (in this way he is similar to Ozu).[31] In *Ordet* there is a certain 'whiteness' to his images that allows the eye to rest and to see the details of the image in its uniqueness.[32] With this precision, Dreyer allows for a different kind of 'real' to emerge that is akin to the poetry of the imagination – the ethical realm in which to create what we see, to invent.

*

In the last scene of *Ordet* we witness the incarnation of grace, and the miraculous. The farmer's son Johannes, who throughout the film believes he is the incarnation of Christ, performs a miracle. He resurrects the beloved Inger, the matron of the family, who dies in childbirth. Inger's devotion to her family and her faith offer resoluteness to the family. Inger is what binds them together. (Throughout the film the madness of Johannes and the emergence of forbidden love between the son and daughter of the warring families is kept in check by Inger's kindness.)

Johannes resurrects Inger after he 'becomes sane' or at least he no longer believes he is the incarnation of Christ. We watch Johannes' 'words' bring Inger back to life; it is the *word* that literally becomes renewed in the film through Inger's resurrection. This unexpected miracle is startling to watch, the unthinkable is enacted in front of us. Just as the characters in the film realise the power of what they have witnessed, we, too, partake in this experience. The miracle unites the everyday and the holy for us in an astonishing way.

Through Inger's resurrection (a resurrection that has never before been filmed in such a light nor perhaps ever will be again?), we are given a strange vision of unity and belonging. The transition from death back to life brings together the disparate belief systems and moral values of the characters, just as it reminds us of the inexplicable and mysterious qualities of this world. In the last words of the film, life inspires hope just as death is remembrance of that which is intangible to us yet enduring; this is Dreyer's spiritual realm.

Weil reminds us:

Man only escapes from the laws of this world in lightning flashes. Instants when everything stands still, instants of contemplation of pure intuition, of mental void, of acceptance of the moral void. It is through such instants that he is capable of the supernatural.

Whoever endures a moment of the void either receives the supernatural bread or falls. It is a terrible risk, but one that must be run – even during the instant when hope fails. But we must not throw ourselves into it.[33]

Dreyer transforms how we might imagine the real, and its conditions. By touching the unthinkable, the miraculous and the everyday, Dreyer brings us nearer to a logic of peace and its proximity, its sacred qualities. It is what Levinas might mean when he says, following Buber, that 'the existence of God is sacred history itself, the sacredness of man's relation to man through which God may pass.'[34] It is this sacred history that belongs to the realm of justice and the good.

We must not forget either, as Durkheim writes, in his studies on the elementary forms of religious life, that miracles in different historical times were not seen as marvellous events of a purely supernatural order. They were beautiful or terrible spectacles that demonstrated the efficacy of time and the power of the sacred:

> ... the miraculous interventions which the ancients attributed to their gods were not seen as miracles in the modern sense of the word. They were beautiful, rare, or terrible spectacles, objects of surprise and wonder; they were not seen as glimpses into a mysterious world closed to reason.[35]

gentleness

So far we have discussed a different moral and aesthetic response to violence. Bachelard has pointed out that the phenomenology of perception must stand aside for a *phenomenology of creative imagination*. In this realm, we respond to the world in its time and in its place. We can see its depths and possibilities. We can imagine the real.

The world, then, can be 'dreamed'; it is a different order of seeing, of myth and storytelling. This dreaming requires a method of looking, a looking without attachment to objects and things, but a look that asks us to consider the time of the world and the time of experience. Bachelard notes:

> Gentleness of seeing while admiring, pride of being admired, those are human bonds. But they are active, in both directions, in our admiration of the world. The world wishes to see itself; the world lives in an active curiosity with ever open eyes. In uniting mythological dreams (*songes*), we can say: *The Cosmos is an Argus*. The Cosmos, a sum of beauties, is

an Argus, a sum of ever open eyes. Thus the theorem of the reverie of vision is translated to the cosmic level: everything that shines sees, and there is nothing in the world which shines more than a look.[36]

*

True songs of peace resonate with the power of generosity, gentleness and kindness without hypocrisy; it is a hope and courage of a different kind. Through grace and courage we can see in a new and different light for all that has been forsaken or grieved. Without grace we lose the deeper connexions of yearning, hope and peace that are the potential of this world and its dreaming. In *Wings of Desire*, the character of Homer speaks of this yearning:

> The world seems to be dawning away,
> but I tell my story, like in the very beginning, in
> my sing-song that keeps me going,
> through my narration
> spared from the rough-and-tumble of the present
> and saved for the future.
>
> No more explaining at large as in the old days,
> back and forth through the centuries.
> I can barely think from one day to another.
> My heroes are no longer the warriors and kings,
> but the things of peace,
> each one as good as the other.
>
> *Die Welt scheint zu verdämmern,*
> *doch ich erzähle, wie am Anfang,*
> *in meinem Singsang, der mich aufrechterhält,*
> *durch die Erzählung verschont von den Wirren der Jetztzeit*
> *und geschont für die Zukunft.*
>
> *Aus ist es mit dem Weitausholen wie früher,*
> *vor und zurück durch die Jahrhunderte.*
> *Kann nur noch von einem Tag zum andern denken. Meine*
> *Helden sind nicht mehr die Krieger und Könige, sondern die*
> *Dinge des Friedens, eins so gut wie das andere.*

Ground Zero, New York, 8 November 2001
(Wim Wenders)

Go, go, go, said the bird: human kind
Cannot bear very much reality.
Time past and time future
What might have been and what has been
Point to one end, which is always present.

                                              T.S. Eliot

5

Which Future of Seeing?

Drawing on previous chapters, we explore how to create conditions for peace by thinking together *with* technology; how technology and its creative use can change our habitual ways of looking at the world. We consider how to re-engage our senses, memories and habits to transform those habits, to create virtues that involve humility and grace as well as the stillness of courage, in order to do justice to the magnitude of peace. We look at filmmakers, photographers, painters, writers and poets whose language or *teckne* provide some virtues and conditions of peace; that is, past virtues for future ways of seeing.

We investigate then some techniques that give us access to the sacred, the qualities and conditions that help us to become aware of the world and each other and open possibilities for a genuine dialogue that can emerge to shape reality, not destroy it.

*

speed

Today, images are everywhere. Never before have there been so many images circulating around the globe. The lightning speed at which images move changes how we see and how events are registered and understood. As a result, there is an altered sense of space, time and memory, and how we constitute individual and cultural identity.

Speed and technology have created new geographies and transnational spaces. French philosopher Paul Virilio argues that in this world order, perception and destruction have become interchangeable.[1] He suggests that there is a direct correlation between military technology and the development of the camera and cinema technology; in this logic of perception war technologies have altered relations to space and time, how we understand the world and perceive it. Power is everywhere and nowhere. He argues that since direct vision in combat has disappeared and one-to-one combat has been replaced by remote military strategy, the route of perception has been a struggle between visibility and invisibility, surveillance and camouflage. We note how these changes in perception are leading to more destructive forces instead of forming creative energies in the use and view of technology.

Italian filmmaker Michelangelo Antonioni had confidence that technological progress would allow for the invention of new images and societies; he saw the future of cinema as science fiction. In Wim's 1982 documentary film *Room 666*, he questioned a number of his colleagues about the future of cinema, and new technology. In that context, Antonioni said:

> Of course, I'm just as worried as anyone else about the future of cinema as we know it. We're attached to it, because it gave us so many ways of saying what we felt and thought we had to say. But as the spectrum of new technical possibilities gets wider, that feeling will eventually disappear. There probably always was that discrepancy between the present and the unimaginable future. Who knows what houses are going to look like in the future – the structures we see when we look out the window probably won't even exist tomorrow. We shouldn't think of the immediate future either, but of the distant future; we must concern ourselves with the kind of world that a future race of humans will inhabit.
>
> . . . I've always been someone who tried to adapt to whatever forms of expression coped best with the contemporary world. I've used video on one of my films; I've experimented with colour, and I've painted reality. The technique was crude, but it represented some kind of advance. I want to go on experimenting.
>
> It's not an easy thing to talk about the future of cinema . . .
>
> Already in *Deserto rosso*, I was looking at the question of adapting – adapting to new technologies, to the polluted air we'll probably have to breathe. Even our physical bodies will probably evolve – who can say in what ways? The future will probably present itself with a ruthlessness we can't yet imagine.
>
> My sense is this: it won't be all that hard to turn us into new people, better used to dealing with the new technologies.[2]

The question is: How will we remember and what cultures will evolve in a technological world? While technology and human culture have always co-existed, how we manage that relationship is what is at stake today. For German philosopher Martin Heidegger, the question concerning technology involves the illumination and piety of thought as well as its danger; therefore

which future of seeing? 135

the stakes are twofold: technology as part of human life and culture can enable the cultivation of the future in the revealing of truth, or technology can lead to destructiveness.[3] In a different way, David Bohm wrote that if technology evolves by a certain 'literalness' – that is, if technology becomes the stand-in for reality or its reflection – we lose the sense of participation or partaking in the 'whole' universe and its implicate order.[4] For Bohm, this issue is not necessarily a metaphysical question, rather it involves the very molecular relations of unfolding time and space and human creativity and human potential for change.[5]

In Heidegger's writings on technology he often cites the German poet Friedrich Hölderlin's line, 'poetically man dwells'. Heidegger calls on the Greek word and philosophical concept of *poiesis*, which means making/creating, and *teckne*, which suggests art or skill. He saw the implications of technology as both creative and artful in orientation just like the human capacity for thought. This *teckne* is where the hope for the future lies. Hölderlin's work searched for the sacredness of god and men, for Heidegger he looked at the mystery that could unfold in the skilful use of technology. Both poet and philosopher believed that the holy could appear in new and still unanticipated forms.

How do we think of technology, the new and still unanticipated forms of the 'holy' and its artful orientation?

air

In Roland Barthes' last and most personal book, *Camera Lucida*, he speaks of the photograph as the medium of love and death, and of the history of photography as a creative enterprise.[6] He notes that the richness and the aliveness of the photograph occurs between the materiality of the technology and its alchemy.[7] He writes:

> It seems that in Latin 'photograph' would be said 'imago lucis opera expressa'; which is to say: image revealed, 'extracted', 'mounted', 'expressed' (like the juice of a lemon) by the action of light. And if Photography belonged to a world with some residual sensitivity to myth, we should exult over the richness of the symbol: the loved body is immortalized by the mediation of a precious metal, silver (monument and luxury); to which we might add the notion that this metal, like all metals of Alchemy, is alive.[8]

For Barthes, the photographic image has various codes, but what he discovered by chance was the 'air' of a photograph, its uniqueness following his mother's death. Looking through old photographs, he found a photo of his mother as a young girl standing next to her brother, the 'Winter Garden Photograph' he called it. This early photo of his mother 'pricked' him in his grief (what Barthes would call the 'punctum'); what he found was not her identity, but something else – between the image of his mother and his memory of her he saw the gestures of her hands, those hands showed a kindness, and her spirit came alive through this kindness in a unique and 'airy' way.

Something altogether different emerged for Barthes: rather than knowing or objectifying the memory of her, her presence came alive through his loving look and response to the image. It was what he called the 'impossible science of the unique being' – that is, his mother was a 'Mother' in a cultural sense like all mothers represented, but what he saw was a radiant, irreducible core, 'my mother', the grace of her 'being an individual soul' who radiated through the image. This image was:

> 'Not a just image, just an image', Godard says. But my grief wanted a just image, an image which would be both justice and accuracy – *justesse*: just an image, but a just image. Such, for me, was the Winter Garden Photograph.[9]

The 'just image' is the 'very space of love, its music'. And Barthes reminds us that the duration of the image suggests that 'Every photograph is a certificate of presence.'[10]

Today how we might understand a 'just image', what we value as special and unique, has altered. With the rapid circulation of images there is a 'derealisation' of space and time. Nowadays 'screens' of all kinds confront us, mobile technology is replacing our face-to-face communication and intimacy, our innermost feelings and desires are communicated through different screens. How we inhabit the world has changed and with it our sense of place and of the surrounding world. Digital photography and digital (re)production can make the 'transience of life', its enduring moments obsolete, since we no longer have to be present to the event or the 'fact' of the world, present to the moment in which life unfolds. As John Berger writes in previous times, to *look* was to commune with the world and its mystery, the awesome and beautiful struggle with the necessity of place, and experience.

What we find today is that people no longer have the patience for detail or stillness, to *really look*. As American author Susan Sontag has written, the 'shock' of images of war or other atrocities may become familiarised to the point that people no longer 'look', or as she says, people may still look, but they do not have the skilful means to see and understand.[11]

Maybe we need to reconsider, then, how we look at the world, how we let the world speak to us?

*

places are in peace

I've photographed remote locations on this planet,
from the deepest Australian desert to the American West,
from the heart of Africa to Armenia.
But I'm not only attracted to faraway places.
I've taken pictures in my own city of Berlin,
in New York or on skyscrapers in Sao Paolo.

What I did in all these places
was to look for their company.
I tried to just be there,
lose myself in those spaces
and listen to them, as much as possible.
Yes, just listen.
One can do that.
We have that ability.
We call it 'a sense of place'.

In ancient times
that was a much more developed human perception than today.
It was one of our senses,
like seeing, tasting, touching or smelling.
People depended on it for survival.
Too often today,
our navigation systems have replaced that capacity.
Nowadays it is actually a human propensity in danger of disappearance,
a sense in the process of going to waste.
It's being replaced by Google Earth and Tom Toms.

Just sit by a river and let it flow by for a while.
The river starts talking to you.
Its presence gets strong and convincing.
Its time superimposes itself on your own sense of time.
It tells you to calm down
and become part of its flow.
'Listen!' the river says.
Before you know it,
the waves splashing onto the stones or the sand in front of you

will have stories to tell.
After all, that river saw history.
We always think that we are the only ones witnessing the past ...

Or just walk into a forest,
come to a clearing and sit down among the trees.
No, it does not have to be redwood trees,
it can be your local birch, pine or palm.
These trees will make you go quiet.
You don't have to hug them.
Just lean your back against one of them and wait.
Listen to their language,
the wind, the birds, the rustle,
the cracking of branches ...

Just sit on an empty beach
and watch the waves,
or walk over those pebbles and stones for a while.
Get into the rhythm of the surf.
Look at the shells and clams
being washed ashore
and being pulled back out into the water.
This is a mighty language.
A cacophony of voices ...
Or spend a night in the desert,
sleeping under the sky.
Sit in a cathedral,
or under a bridge,
walk through a valley
or climb a mountain ...

You'll no longer have any trouble accepting
that places talk to you.
It is just that we are too used to being the talkers.
That has become a habit.
We've lost the ability to listen.

It might be easier to accept
that rivers, forests, oceans talk
than any old house,
any rolling hill,
any street corner,

which future of seeing?

any wall,
any abandoned ruin,
any gas station
or ... you name it.
But that is just what I'm convinced of.
Places speak to us.
All of them!
They have messages,
they tell stories.
Some are sad,
some are hopeful,
some are joyful.
And, yes, some have stopped talking.
They're all talked out.
They gave up on us.

I have that very distinct feeling sometimes
when I get to places
that have been eroded by tourism.
They have often shut up.
They have been stared at and photographed
by so many blind eyes and deaf ears
that they have given up talking,
by a sense of offence, insult, violation.

Last time I came to Monument Valley, for instance,
a site I have visited often, in awe,
I soon fled in dread.
I had the feeling the place had clammed up,
had decided to wrap itself in secrecy
and fall into silence.

But that is the exception.
Places *do* want to talk, normally,
and they do open up, if you are patient.
I love to listen to them.
A camera then can become a recording device
(eventually, not right away),
to capture the place's story, or history,
and gather details of its account.

The entire Earth is talking to us,
not only Nature ('mother nature') –
water, plants, trees and rocks,
plains, hills, valleys and oceans –
but also what we've constructed on it.
Roads, buildings, bridges, signs ...

Anyway,
whenever I listened
(better: when I allowed myself to listen,
when I was privileged to listen,
when I was invited to listen),
I never found any other message,
never heard any other sound,
never eavesdropped on any other stories
than peaceful ones.

Places are in peace.
They know nothing else.
We know it,
the ... 'something else',
the 'absence of peace',
the 'war',
the 'violence',
the 'whatshallwecallit':
that is the reversal of peace.
We don't even have a proper word for it!
'Unpeace' ...

We seem to bring it with us,
this 'other element',
introduce invasion and destruction everywhere,
and turn landscapes into battlefields and minefields.

That was not what God meant in Genesis 1.28
when he said to man:
'Be fruitful, and multiply,
and replenish the Earth,
and subdue it.'

But I don't want to talk about *us*,
I want to talk about places

which future of seeing? 141

and their relentless and unbroken ability
(capacity, talent, gift, will ...)
to convey and talk of peace.

And maybe I have to go to the extreme to make that point
and to convince you.
(If necessary ...)

I once visited Ground Zero.
That was in October of 2001.
Like all of humanity I had seen the towers fall,
with unbelieving, hurting eyes.
Like for billions of people
those images had invaded my dreams,
had carved themselves into my brain,
even if I would have rather wanted to delete them,
like all of us, from our memory.

I felt I had to see for myself
in order to live with these mental images again,
to not have them live inside me like cancer cells.

I flew to New York.
The entire downtown zone was blocked off.
After the first onslaught of reporters and cameramen,
the mayor of New York had decided
to let nobody enter the area any more.
It was still a mass grave,
a smouldering hell hole
with a cloud of acidy smell hanging over it.

One man was allowed to have access and take pictures,
as the 'mayor's official photographer',
and he did this with dedication and utter commitment:
Joel Meyerowitz.
Every day his camera witnessed the work of the firemen,
and the crews that searched the debris, stone by stone,
and slowly started to take the mountain of rubble away.

Joel understood my desire to see for myself
and helped me to get into the forbidden area.
One day, he just took me along with him.

He had made a badge for me, a copy of his own, as his assistant.
The guards let us through.

For one whole morning, until noon,
we walked around together,
saw what we saw
and took pictures.
Every second of these hours is engraved into my mind.

It was still dawn when we started.
The silhouette of the exterior wall
of the World Trade Center's entrance hall
rose sharply against the sky.
There was smoke coming from the ground.
Below, the fire was still smoldering,
like lava at the bottom of a volcano.

We walked and worked in silence.
Joel knew most of the firemen and workers,
and greeted them by their names.
Nobody spoke loudly.
There was a common sense of reverence and awe.
The crews went through every heap of stones and rubble
with immense care,
always alert to finding traces of bodies.

Every now and then there was an alarm signal,
because something had been found somewhere, and
then everybody shut up for a moment.
One could not help feeling like in the ruins of a big church,
a mighty cathedral that had burned to the ground.

And then the sun came up.
It was still early in the morning.
Ground Zero was surrounded by skyscrapers,
so the early sun could not shine directly into the hole,
into that huge wound on the ground.
But the sun was reflected
from the glass surfaces of the adjoining buildings,
its rays piercing through the smoke and the mist.

We had walked with our gaze fixed to the ground.

I lifted my eyes up, for the first time.
And Joel and I stood there in silence.
What we saw was hard to believe.

Joel shook his head and mumbled something
that he had come for weeks now
but never had seen anything like it.
And as it was only lasting for a few moments,
I raised my panoramic camera
and took the picture:

Of sheer beauty.

I know this is hard to say.
And almost impossible to believe.
It sounds blasphemous.
But I cannot say it any other way.
I would have to lie.
There was beauty.
And peace.

For a moment,
the place spoke all on its own,
through the sun, the surrounding buildings,
the rubble and the smoldering ground,
the bulldozers and cranes,
the smoke and the rays of light.

Its message was:
Something horrible *took place* here.
It took *me*.
I *am* that place to which it happened,
I do know better than anyone else!
The blood of all these people who died here
has soaked into my skin,
and their cries are forever echoing in the air above me.
But I, the place,
with the sun as my witness right now,
want to tell you:
let this not be in vain!
Let death not create more death!
Revenge will not make sense of the sacrifice

that happened here.
Only forgiveness.
Let this be a place of peace,
of rest,
of healing.

I walked away from Ground Zero with the firm conviction
that September 11 should be seen as a turning point in history.
The place had shown it to me
and has demonstrated powerfully
that time would heal.
A new era, new politics of peace
could start *here*.

Unfortunately,
events took the opposite direction.
Politics of the United States of America were such
that they used Ground Zero as a war symbol.
And what a senseless war it became,
built on lies to begin with!
And how inflationary even the use of the word 'war'.
'War on terrorism' was (and is) a contradiction in terms.
Time revealed the lies and the futility of war.

In my book,
Ground Zero still maintains its message.
It is still waiting to be heard.

*

light

If we *really look*, every moment has potential to transform the violence that assaults us; herein lies the power of invention and choice we spoke of in Chapter 2. Images of violence do not belong to another world or to the past, to remote places and events, they exist – a photograph becomes a 'certificate of presence'. In many ways, it is not empathy that is required here nor even sympathy, but the connection *with* suffering, to be a 'sincere' witness for others.[12] This witnessing does not put others at a distance, nor does it seek testimony, redemption or solution, rather it begs questions

such as: 'What needs to be done here?', 'What is our responsibility?' Or simply: 'How can I help?'
The photography of Sebastião Salgado touches the 'duration' we speak of; his photographs invite us to be with the child, mother, father, husband, wife, woman, man, son, daughter in the war zone or the refugee camp. Instead of remoteness and distance between others and ourselves in his photographs, there is a connection, something 'pricks' us as Barthes might say, wounds us in some way as we move together with others in their reality, not against it. His photographs demonstrate a great patience and love. With Salgado's photographs, when a child or the mother looks at the camera, they are not seeking to identify with the existential question 'Who am I?' – rather they ask of us: 'Who are you?'

pictures of peace

I'm more than impressed
with an effort by one of my favourite photographers on this planet,
Sebastião Salgado.
For decades he took pictures in all parts of the world,
of humankind's suffering and labour,
of war and violence,
of greed and misery ...
We all know his images.

But for the last ten years he has moved on to do the opposite:
to take pictures of our planet
where it is still like God created it.
(Which according to him
applies to more than a third of the Earth's surface.)
GENESIS is the name of his project.
He visited remote tribes in the Amazon, in Africa or Papua New Guinea.
He saw landscapes that were never touched or travelled.
He photographed animals in the jungle and in Polar regions.
He took pictures of our planet
as if he could have made them 'in the beginning' ...

He is truly tapping into time's memory bank.
His hope is
that these images of absolute peace
will help counterbalance the onslaught of negative imagery
that we are exposed to on a day-to-day basis.

Genesis Project
(© Sebastião Salgado/Amazonas, NB Pictures)

Salgado's work is in black and white.
For me that corresponds entirely to his mission.
Today, a black and white image is an abstraction from reality.
The world we constantly see is governed by violence and greed.
And it mostly presents itself in glorious colours.
The world Salgado shows us is 'behind' the familiar front.
His b/w images show the essence of things.
What IS and what will remain.
Yes, peace is largely invisible.
War always demands centre stage.

*

Images of violence that constantly assault the senses need to be envisioned through the duration of photography, the very 'imaginary' of the image – that is, a change in how we see. Bachelard writes that 'brilliant photographers know how to give duration to their snapshots, very exactly a *duration of reverie*.'[13] This duration is what opens an image to its radiance, it is what can deepen and magnify an experience, and in terms of violence it is the creative means to respond to it (see Chapter 4).

Bachelard notes that we must think of the corresponding word for imagination as the *imaginary* not image: 'the value of an image is measured by the extent of its imaginary radiance.' This is an invitation to consider the dynamic relations of an image and its transforming qualities, the very power of the human psyche and its imaginary. And when we experience the depth of an image, its uniqueness, we experience moments of infinitude. Buber writes: 'And just as a prayer is not in time but time in prayer, sacrifice not in space but space in sacrifice, and to reverse the relation is to abolish reality.'[14]

In a different way, American painter Edward Hopper achieves this with light: through the starkness of his images, of his interior and exterior shots, it is almost as if he casts light on an American soul of the time, its concerns and sensibility. By removing most of the detail from a street scene or a room the colours and people are illuminated in a harsh and cruel light. At the same time, there is a softness and vulnerability that shines through his paintings; the light becomes the very imagination of the image, its intuition and life.

Let us consider how, as John Berger notes, in a world full of false images and distractions, to try and paint 'is an act of resistance instigating hope'.[15] Every painting demonstrates a certain mystery and dialogue with the world. It is with this hope that we can refresh our senses and listen to what our eyes tell us. As previously discussed, this is a 'phenomenology of creative imagination' that engages the imagination and the duration of the world, 'making us create what we see' (see Chapter 4). Bachelard writes this is an opening to a beautiful world, to beautiful worlds of enchantment, imagination and vision.

Street Corner in Butte, Montana, USA, 2003
(Wim Wenders)

radiance

The great painters all teach us to see.
That goes for abstract visionaries, of course,
as well as for realist painters.
Rothko leads us to different layers of perception
than Vermeer, Beuys, Klee or Twombly,
but we don't want to miss any of their 'insights',
in the very sense of the word.

I was always strangely drawn to those painters
who remained 'figurative' (for lack of a better word)
when the entire art world around them had turned
into a different direction.
That goes for the enigmatic Balthus
as for the great Beckmann,
but especially for those American painters
who stoically continued their path,
even when their art seemed to have become completely obsolete
against the abstract currents or the onslaught of Pop Art.
(Maybe because I find 'defending reality' more heroic
than inventing a new one.)
I'm talking of Edward Hopper here, of course,
but even more so of a painter
who has not caught all that much attention outside of America
and who has often been put in the wrong context:
Andrew Wyeth.

For me he is the most courageous defender
of a 'realist' concept in the twentieth century,
with an extraordinary vision of things.
He has been classified, terribly, as a 'primitive painter',
or discarded as an 'American patriotic painter',
the 'hero artist of agrarian America'.
'Regional Art' was yet another discriminating category that he was put in.
Yet, if you discard all these kinds of pigeonholes
and just look at the work without a predisposition,
you might be as stunned as I was, and am.

Andrew Wyeth was a radical.
He lived entirely withdrawn, outside of any school or grouping.

(He got his formation from his father, the painter N.C. Wyeth.)
He perfected a style and technique of painting
that had its heyday in the Renaissance: egg tempera,
which was mostly replaced by oil painting since then
and largely forgotten in the twentieth century.
Dürer painted this way, for instance, whom Wyeth admired a lot.
This old technique, and the skill that he acquired in it,
allowed for an incredible richness of detail and texture
for Wyeth's large canvasses
on which he worked for months at a time,
and of which he didn't produce more than two or three a year.

Still, Andrew Wyeth had a huge output,
because he also perfected the art of watercolours
which he used for taking notes and for pre-studies.
'Dry brush' became his trademark,
which, again, he brought to such a perfection
that it makes you stare at these works in disbelief.
Watercolours often have the connotation of being fleeting,
'swooshy' and somehow only sketch-work.
Wyeth's watercolours are the opposite.
He painted snowy landscapes, for instance,
that caught the texture and the light of snow
so that you might think he just photographed those places
(same for his portraits, for that matter)
and only at the edges you see in wonder
how it all frayed into nothing but paint and brushstrokes.

But it is not because of his mastery
and the most brilliant use of painting techniques
that I'm in awe of Wyeth
and convinced he is a great teacher of seeing
who can indeed help us in the quest
of finding a new access to perceiving peace.
I'm drawn to his work for different reasons.

Wyeth lived in a remote area of Pennsylvania.
He lived there for six months a year,
but restricted his 'painting range'
to a couple of square miles around his house and his studio.
He couldn't care less about the rest of the world.
For the other six months of the year

he went to an even more remote place on the coast of Maine,
where he painted again only the most immediate vicinity
and the people he found there.
Fall and winter paintings in Pennsylvania,
spring and summer paintings in Maine.
That was his entire painter's life.
And he painted all the time,
even returned to his studio at night
to stare at the half-finished canvasses in darkness.

He painted fields, barns, houses, interiors.
And he portrayed simple people,
his neighbours, workers, drifters.
With obsession he painted details like branches and grass,
or a mussel on the beach.
He loved to paint snow
and was attracted by everything white.

His most famous painting
(the equivalent to the other icon of the twentieth century,
Hopper's *Nighthawks*)
is called *Christina's World*.
You probably know it:
A woman sitting in a field, in the foreground, left to the centre,
her back to us,
at the bottom of a wide and altogether empty hill,
at the top of which stands a simple two-storey country house
with a barn it its side.
There is a huge void and barrenness
between the woman and that house.
Her hair is slightly blowing in the wind.
And you also feel the breeze in the grass
that is stretched out in front of her, up to the house.
Andrew Wyeth painted nothing but the brown grass for several months.
You see each and every blade of grass.
The texture of the woman's dress, her skin, her hair,
every thing is of unbelievable vividness.
Although it is painted, it is not 'static'.
There is an immediacy to the painter's regard, a freshness,
that you think you only know from photo 'snapshots'.
That woman might turn around in the next second . . .
She looks young and vibrant.

Wyeth has painted Christina Olson for more than twenty years,
over and over again,
in that simple house on the hill, which is hers,
in her kitchen, at her doorstep, knitting, caressing her kitten . . .
He has done elaborate tempera portraits of her
and countless watercolour sketches.

He has really immersed into her being,
has really 'seen' her, 'recognised' her.
has done all he can to depict her in all the glory of her existence.
Yes, one can say that he glorified her,
that he showed her 'for all eternity'
as who she was and how she was.
I'm deeply moved by this effort and the dedication of a painter
to bring the existence of one person to light,
to convey her being, her essence, her presence to canvasses.

(Since the nineteenth and twentieth centuries
all of that can be preserved in photography, sure,
but still more solidly in painting,
where the eye of the beholder,
together with his hand and his affection,
is so much more 'involved'
and where there is so much more at stake,
considering the invested life-time of both painter and model.)

You don't have to know in order to appreciate this painting
(but then again it broke my heart when I read it)
that Christina was paralysed and unable to move her legs,
and when she looks at her house in the distance
in that painting *Christina's World*
it means she would have had to crawl to that observation point
and she would have to crawl back to her home.
And she was an old woman
when Wyeth made that painting . . .
In fact the whole 'reality' of the painting is invented.
Wyeth caught a glimpse of Christina once, from a window,
crawling around the house,
and he painted her as the young woman
(whom he did not know),
when she was still able to walk.

which future of seeing? 153

The gracefulness of that young figure is stunning.
We can only see her from the back
(and maybe we wondered a bit about her skinny arms and legs),
and her face we can only imagine
(but we imagine it beautiful)
with all the inner beauty that her figure suggests to us.

This is a sudden momentary glimpse Wyeth painted,
but yet, the longer you watch it,
the more timeless the painting becomes.
It seems to happen outside of time ...

The 'Great Peace' that Martin Buber speaks about
it is all there in this picture,
and more than a hint of it.
You see the need for it, the yearning for it.
That indescribable, tremendous peace,
here we can take a look at it.

There is another painting of Wyeth's
that immediately comes to my mind.
It is a 'still life', so to speak,
and fulfils every possible definition of that expression
and those two words of 'still' (as in 'rest, quietness')
but also 'still' as in 'I'm still hungry'
and 'life', of course,
with all its many connotations,
especially as 'life' involves us *and* the picture.
It is the very realm in which all seeing is taking place,
it is the most precious dimension
(and the most inexplicable one):
the mystery of us, and things, and places being there, in time.
'Life' is both 'time' and 'presence'.
So this painting *Wind from the Sea*
incorporates all the countless reverberations of 'still life' for me.

It shows nothing but a look out of the window.
Yes, we are in Christina's house again.
We (indeed, *we*) look through an open window,
in front of which a curtain is blowing,
out into an empty landscape.
A curved path is leading to the distant sea.

Again, Wyeth painted the lace of that curtain for months,
and the momentary and utterly elusive split second of a gust of wind
that gently moved it.
Again, as in *Christina's World*, there is the instant and eternity.
Wyeth teaches us, or helps us, to see both.
And maybe that's the greatest lesson
for our damaged and limited perception in need of guidance
to learn again to be in the moment and outside of its time.
He makes us see the wonder of both,
which is exactly what our daily avalanche of images is hiding.
The more pictures we see,
the less we see how extraordinary every slice of life is.

Losing that ability is opening the flood doors to arbitrariness,
which makes us an easy prey to images of violence
and the atrocious attraction of war.

Each of Wyeth's paintings is the result (and radiates it)
of a first-hand experience into which he sank very deeply,
and which he succeeded in keeping alive in painting it.
(Which other painter was able to hold on to that ephemeral quality?)
Wyeth once described that the things he painted,
he first saw them only from the corner of his eyes,
and often he only recognised much later
what it was that caught his attention.
And then he brought back that 'accidental moment'
and filled it with an incredible richness of detail,
made it dense and full,
yet did not lose that flash of the first innocent look.

He came to that room on the upper floor in Christina's house
where nobody had been in ages,
where the air was stuffy and hot,
and he opened the window,
and that first gust of wind that came in,
that was what he wanted to paint!
Miraculously he painted also the stuffiness of the room,
and the quality of the sea air coming in.

Sure, Wyeth paints 'reality',
and you might even be inclined to call it a hyper-reality,
because of its intensity and unbelievable amount of detail.

which future of seeing?

But it would be wrong to reduce him to being a 'realistic painter'.
His style should not at all be categorised as 'realism'.
That's not what he is after.
Rather like an abstract painter,
he is interested in what is behind the surface of what he sees.
He wants to uncover in (and through) his work
the essence of a person, or a place, or an object.
In order to find it, he goes about with almost surgical precision,
and by investing an enormous amount of time and patience,
only that he happens to have chosen other means and tools
than his abstract colleagues,
and that it is the visible world he is interested in, after all,
not any interior space or invention.

Any depiction of 'reality', it seems to me,
is directly linked to the present tense and to the moment.
Wyeth is looking for a different time zone.
Even if he fights hard
to maintain the freshness and the spontaneity of his first glance,
he then works even harder to put that instant into a different measure.
Timelessness is what he is after.
He somehow tries to install 'eternity' into his canvasses.
Or at least, in a portrait: a lifetime,
even the generations that lead this person
to be what he (or she) is in the eyes of the painter.
In an object, Wyeth paints the mystery
that this thing, or plant, or animal, exists as such.
And, in a landscape, he tries to encapsulate the ages,
the accumulated time that weighs on the place.
The house or interior will show its wornness,
every trace of its use or abuse.
Time stands still, the world materialises in utter clarity
and as a sheer marvel.

You see this most plainly in his watercolour sketches.
There is a chaos of wild and abstract brush strokes,
and out of this whirly mess, an object peels out,
or a landscape manifests itself.
In the transition between disorder and the appearance of the world
you see that it is the very same paint and the same brush strokes
that let reality emerge from the hubbub
('*tohuwabohu*' is the Hebrew word for it in Genesis)

as if he had sucked it out of it,
or better: as if he had put all the atoms back together in the right way.

So Wyeth sees out of the corner of his eyes first,
remembers later what he saw,
then sees again, immerses himself,
penetrates, transcends and reconstructs,
thus shows us both the reflection of that first glance
and what lies behind it, and what lasts;
he reveals that person,
but also his relation to him, or her.
That also goes for things and places.
He gives us a whole chronicle, an account of time,
a narrative of his subject.

Critics have reproached him for being 'anecdotic',
of giving too much context instead of just the surface,
as the art world demanded at that time (and still does).
Wyeth never bothered.
He was a storyteller as well,
he wanted to be one,
he needed to be one to see more completely.
He was certain that it needed all that setting,
all that framework to a portrait, a still life or a landscape.

And that is why I consider him so crucial.
We've unlearned that complexity in seeing
which is mostly an act of first sight for us.
(And often we don't have any other choice.)
Wyeth teaches us the second and third sight.
He says: 'Look at all the responsibility that is involved in the act of seeing.
Look at the pleasures of digging deeper.
Look at the rewards of putting yourself
into very "presence" of a person, or a thing, or a landscape.
Let the glance out of the corner of your eye
lead you to really look and recognise
and see each other, the world and its radiance,
with more durability,
with more sincerity,
with more pleasure,
and with more communion happening.'

which future of seeing? 157

Well, painters are not the only such teachers for
the act of seeing ...

rhythm

When Robert Bresson reflected on his filmic techniques, he wrote: 'Have a painter's eye. The painter creates by looking.'[16] His films show with urgency the necessity to act in response to cruelty and violence as well as how to *look* at the world and our relations to it. Movies – as he called them, as distinct from cinematography – distract us, they are forms of entertainment. For Bresson, movies have too many 'screens' – they block out reality rather than demanding that we respond to it. These screens are movie devices such as plot, camera work, editing and music that manipulate our attention as well as 'actors'. He believed in the neutrality of his 'models', as he called his actors, they communicate the necessity of the image. Bresson writes: 'Human Models: movement from the exterior to the interior (Actors: movement from the interior to the exterior)'.[17] We might consider Bresson's cinematographic method as 'retouching the real', a matter of grace and spiritual unity of a different kind.

Bresson's films confront the sacred elements of the everyday. He invents a filmic rhythm that gives a unity to otherwise disparate events, most often spiritual and social disenfranchisement, but this unity comes about by looking at the detail and small elements that make up the 'whole' and the relationship to it. Bresson quotes the French philosopher Blaise Pascal on this point: 'A town or countryside at a distance is a town, a countryside; but as one approaches, those are houses, trees, tiles, leaves, grasses, ants, ants' legs, to infinity.'[18]

For Bresson, it is rhythm: the relationship of sound and image that creates a 'pure relationship' between things, people and the world, a certain necessity that allows viewers to participate in his films, but also puts us in a 'state of revolt'. Rhythm can demonstrate, disrupt, intervene and transform our vision; essentially, rhythm belongs to everyone and no one, and it is the rhythms of life that connect us as well as tear us apart. Fundamentally, we grasp each other (and meaning) before anything else through rhythm; words and images resonate with a rhythm. Bresson achieves this rhythm through his form and technique. He writes:

> I attach enormous importance to form. Enormous. And I believe that form leads to the rhythm. Now the rhythms are all powerful. Access to the audience is before everything else a matter of rhythm.[19]

And:

> The true is not encrusted in the living persons and real objects you use. It is an air of truth that their images take on when you set them together in a certain order. Vice versa, the air of truth their images take on when you set them together in a certain order confers on these persons and objects a reality.[20]

If we return to Bresson's *Au hasard Balthazar* that we discussed in the previous chapter, we can see through the juxtaposition of sound and image how the wheels of a cart bring into focus human neglect and greed as well as the donkey's humility and grace. Eventually, as the cart topples over, human exploitative practices are brought to the fore. The juxtaposition of sound and image tells the eye how to 'listen' – the awesome and terrible events that encapsulate the world – by interrupting our usual ways of looking at it.

Bresson wrote that he did not make beautiful images, but necessary ones. Beauty in this sense comes out of necessity, the experience and the conditions that the world presents to us or, in other words what is 'fitting'. Justice, fitting and beauty in their derivation share a historical relationship: each points to what is *fitting* in all aspects of life that embrace ethical as well as practical and aesthetic sensibilities. It is in this way that his films generate a strange durability and radiance even in the darkest moments of human actions and choice.

vision

In Antonioni's 1970 film *Zabriskie Point* there is a momentary pause in the film just before the riot police fire on student activists. This moment is crucial as it shows two distinct points, firstly the propensity toward the real of such a moment – that is, the moment of stillness before the assault of fire – and secondly, as Antonioni comments:

> I'm convinced that a policeman does not have death on his mind when he enters a university or faces a mob. He has too many things to do, too many orders to follow. The policeman is not thinking of death anymore than a hunter is thinking of the death of a bird ... If the policeman gave some thought to death he probably wouldn't shoot.[21]

Antonioni's films work with the rhythm and pace of life, this rhythm works with the habits and tendencies of human relationships. What we see, then, is a cinematic rhythm that offers a vision of America, or post-war Italy, or the view of one man's journey and stolen identity in *The Passenger*.[22] His films show the movement of bodies and spaces, gestures and feelings that are often the result of the 'weariness' of the body and the effects of new technologies on everyday life.

He writes:

> A filmmaker is a man like any other; and yet his life is not the same. *Seeing* is for us a necessity. For a painter too the problem is one of seeing: but while for the painter it is a matter of uncovering a static reality, or at least most of a rhythm can be held in a single image, for a director the problem is to catch reality which is never static, is always moving toward or away from the moment of crystallization, and to present this movement, this arriving and moving on, as a new perception.
>
> It is not sound – words, noises, music. Nor is it a picture – landscape, attitudes, gestures. Rather it is an indivisible whole that extends over a duration of its own which determines its very being.[23]

For Antonioni, it is the dimension of time that comes into play, it is in this order of intuition that cinema can acquire a 'new character, no longer merely figurative'. He states:

> The people around us, the places we visit, the events we witness – it is the spatial and temporal relations these have with each other that have meaning for us today, and the tension that is formed between them.[24]

Antonioni, like Ozu, offers through the austerity of his work an aesthetic reappraisal of the human spirit and soul. The action and rhythm of his films demonstrate a patience, a slowness where events often take shape in the time it takes to experience them. Like Ozu, the essential components of a scene are most often in real time, the time it takes for a dialogue to take place or an event to unfold (see Chapter 3).

For instance, the last scene of *The Passenger* is in real time. This scene, which lasts seven minutes, involves the murder of the journalist David Locke (Jack Nicholson), who has stolen the identity of an arms dealer; the camera moves from inside a hotel room to the exterior world outside, and this camera work was made possible with hanging tracks from the ceiling, gyroscopes and a crane. As the audience watches the events unfold in the exterior world, inside the hotel room the murder takes place. The duration of the scene and the camera's remoteness bring us closer to the clandestine murder of the 'arms dealer' in the hotel room. This movement in time and the everydayness of the event makes us look at the scene and each of the characters' relationship to the murder, just as it depicts the invisible elements of violence, its everydayness and human culpability.

Antonioni's slowness, patience and starkness in the last scenes give a way of relating to the situation without sentiment, but with the event as it unfolds. In *The Passenger*, the accumulation of real time and its pace are what come together in the film so that we cultivate patience for what we see; it is the time of experience. The unity of the film is not its plot, but its rhythm and the quality of the vision. The slowness and pace work against the desire for speed and entertainment, to break habits of seeing that action films and high drama simply cannot.

Just before the end sequence of *The Passenger*, there is a dialogue between the two main characters that gives insight into Antonioni's vision, and how we see:

Locke: What do you see?
Woman: A little boy and an old woman. They are having an argument about which way to go ...
Locke: You shouldn't have come.
(*some time passes*)
What can you see now?
Woman: A man scratching his shoulder. A kid throwing stones, and dust. It's very dusty here.
Isn't it funny how things happen?
All the shapes we make.
Wouldn't it be terrible to be blind?
Locke: I know a man who was blind. When he was nearly forty years old he had an operation and regained his sight.
Woman: What was it like?
Locke: At first he was elated. Really High.
Faces, colours, landscapes.
But then everything began to change.
The world was much uglier than he imagined. No one had ever told him how much dirt there was.
How much ugliness.
He noticed ugliness everywhere.
When he was blind he used to cross the street alone with a stick.
After he regained his sight he became afraid. He began to live in darkness.
He never left his room.
After three years he killed himself.

*

Techniques of patience, slowness and stillness can be cultivated. These techniques open up the possibility of listening, hearing, pausing before an action and its consequences. The films of Antonioni, Ozu and Bresson ask us to wait in different ways, to be with a different reality, its rhythms and responsibilities (just as Dreyer 'imagines the real' as we discussed in the previous chapter). And the paintings of Hopper and Wyeth invite us to look at the radiance and eeriness of this world with a certain responsibility, wonder and care. Following Dostoyevsky, this responsibility embraces an artistic as well as ethical responsibility for all humankind. Dostoyevsky notes: 'We are all responsible for all for all men before all, and I more than all others.'[25]

If we return to the scene discussed earlier from *Zabriskie Point*, what might come between the riot police and the student protests could be the essential link of patience, just as the same patience is required between the revolutionary and the gun that fires at the police, as Levinas writes:

> We must recall these virtues of patience not so as to preach a sense of resignation in the face of revolutionary spirit, but so that we can feel the essential link which connects the spirit of patience with true revolution. This revolution comes with great pity. The hand that grasps the weapon must suffer in the very violence of that gesture. To anaesthetize this pain brings the revolutionary to the frontiers of fascism.[26]

roundness

Martin Buber reminds us that the world is of relation and connection; in this world there is no dialectic of seeing rather a whole relation of the world and how we encounter it. This is a phenomenology of experience that is 'round'.

Buber writes:

I consider a tree.

I can look on it as a picture: stiff column in a shock of light, or splash of green shot with the delicate blue and silver of the background.

I can perceive it as a movement: flowing veins on clinging, pressing pith, suck of the roots, breathing of the leaves, ceaseless commerce with earth and air – and the obscure growth itself.

I can classify it in a species and study it as type in its structure and mode of life.

I can subdue its actual presence and form so sternly that I recognise it only as an expression of law – of the laws in accordance with which a constant opposition of forces is continually adjusted, or of those in accordance with which the component substances mingle and separate.

I dissipate it and perpetuate it in number, in pure numerical relation.

In all this the tree remains my object, occupies space and time, and has its nature and constitution.

It can, however, also come about, if I have both will and grace, that in considering the tree I become bound up in relation to it. The tree is now no longer *It*. I have been seized by the power of exclusiveness.

To effect this it is not necessary for me to give up any of the ways in which I consider the tree. There is nothing from which I would have to turn my eyes away in order to see, and no knowledge that I would have to forget. Rather is everything, picture and movement, species and type, law and number, indivisibly united in this event.

Everything belonging to the tree is in this: its form and structure, its colours and chemical composition, its intercourse with the elements and with the stars, are all present in a single whole.

The tree is no impression, no play of my imagination, no value depending on my mood; but it is bodied over against me and has to do with me, as I with it – only in a different way.

Let no attempt be made to sap the strength from the meaning of the relation: relation is mutual.

The tree will have a consciousness, then, similar to our own? Of that I have no experience. But do you wish, through seeming to succeed in it with yourself, once again to disintegrate that which cannot be disintegrated? I encounter no soul or dryad of the tree, but the tree itself.[27]

which future of seeing? 163

Considering Buber's tree, we can see the relation of nature and the whole, its roundness and unity.[28] In his tree, there is unity of presence, of volume, of being. 'Relation is mutual.' Let us consider this: when we move *with* technology and nature rather than being alienated from them and by them, memories, experiences and technologies become sources of inventing that can sharpen vision, give us presence and inspire us. Thinking with technology in a creative sense, the world becomes relational, we work with the world not against it, a relational sense of technology invites a necessary shift in our thinking and imaginations. It opens another dimension where space and time live in us and through us. Instead of being caught in a network of violence that technology can produce by the de-realisation of space and time, we can choose how to respond to the world and creatively invent it.

Bachelard said elsewhere, *being is round*. He writes that the world is 'round around the round being'. He suggests that birds are 'almost' spherical in this living world, he reminds us of the need for this roundness and imaginary. Most often humans are governed by linear thought and reason and enslaved by the shadows that ensue (much like Plato's cave). As Montaigne reminds us, every movement reveals us. There is awareness that is not dictated by the shadows of human thought, but by movement, being and invention.

Rilke writes of this roundedness in his early twentieth-century poem, 'Apprehension':

> In the faded forest is a birdcall
> that seems meaningless in this faded forest.
> And yet the rounded birdcall rests
> in this interim that shaped it,
> wide as a sky upon the faded forest.
> Everything pliantly makes room in the cry:
> The whole landscape seems to lie there soundlessly,
> the great wind seems to nestle inside,
> and time, which wants to move on,
> has, pale and silent, as if it knew things
> for which one has to die,
> risen out of it.

> *Im welken Walde ist ein Vogelruf,*
> *der sinnlos scheint in diesem welken Walde.*
> *Und dennoch ruht der runde Vogelruf*
> *in dieser Weile, die ihn schuf,*
> *breit wie ein Himmel auf dem welken Walde.*
> *Gefügig räumt sich alles in den Schrei:*
> *Das ganze Land scheint lautlos drin zu liegen,*

> *der grosse Wind scheint sich hineinzuschmiegen,*
> *und die Minute, welche weiter will,*
> *ist bleich und still, als ob sie Dinge wüsste,*
> *an denen jeder sterben müsste,*
> *aus ihm herausgestiegen.*[29]

There is a phenomenology of experience that is round when space and time are no longer illusions, but live in us; we experience this all the time, but how can technology give us this experience of unity of volume, space and presence that can transform and sharpen our vision?

another dimension

We had been friends for many years,
the great German choreographer Pina Bausch and I.
Her art had completely blown me away
when I had first seen it in the mid-Eighties,
and ever since we had been talking about making a film together.
Like nobody before her,
Pina had explored the relation between men and women,
without words, just using the language of the human body.
The question of 'who we are'
had always been the subject of all arts,
but here, in Pina's 'dance theatre'
it was asked more directly, more physically, more intimately than ever,
not philosophically or intellectually,
but in an engaging, contagious, popular way,
through motion, 'person to person'.

For me, her work was so amazing and ground-breaking,
so liberating and healing,
and it had such a lasting effect on me,
that I really wanted to 'pass on the virus'
and show this to as many people as possible in a film.

The only question was: *How?!*
I felt my filmmaking tools weren't good enough to do Pina's art justice.
Whatever I imagined that my cameras could do,
there would always be something missing!
I would always be 'outside looking in'.
Like gazing into an aquarium,

which future of seeing? 165

where the dancers were the fish,
my cameras could never be in the water with them.
It was as if an invisible wall stood between Pina's work on stage
and what I could translate onto the screen.

So I hesitated for years, unsure about my filmmaking means.
Pina was patient with me.
'One day you'll find it!' she kept saying.
'You just have to keep on looking.'
I kept searching in my own imagination,
but I never found an answer there.

And then, one day, the solution presented itself to me.
I didn't find it in my soul,
it consisted in a new technology: digital 3D.
All of a sudden I understood
that this was exactly what we had been missing:
an access to another dimension!
'Space' had been what had been missing in my filmmaking grammar.
It was only too obvious,
yet we could not have been thinking about it.
Three-dimensional representation had simply not been accessible.
It had been around, once, in the Fifties,
but that technology then was flawed and had disappeared for good reasons.

Now 3D was available again.
And this *had to be* the language for our film!
It seemed so obvious!
The dancer's realm was *space*.
With every gesture, every step, every movement
they were exploring it, delving into it.
And here was a tool that gave access to their kingdom!
My craft had just been given the missing extra dimension!
Not a small thing, certainly not a gimmick!

For a hundred years cinema had invented splendid tricks
which I loved and cherished (and still do)
to overcome its huge deficit;
it had always made us believe
that 'space' was actually available on the screen.
By moving the camera on tracks, on cars, on helicopters,
by dropping it from planes, by letting it float and fly

– Abel Gance had swung a camera through a room
hanging on a rope, in 1927! –
cinema had created the illusion that it had a grip on 'space',
that it was, indeed, on a 'Space Odyssey'.
But all of its efforts had always ended up on a two-dimensional screen.

Anyway, this ended for me when I saw *U2 3D*, a concert film.
I didn't have much eyes for the film,
I even didn't want to see its flaws,
the figures of Bono and Edge that often looked like cutouts,
the jerky movements sometimes;
after all, this was a predecessor to something bigger to come.
I just saw the *possibilities*!
And the *affinity*!
This new medium (and I took it for granted it was going to be one)
was *made* to represent dance, to bring out its best.
And somehow I even felt it was also going to work the other way around:
dance was going to bring out the best in 3D …

Pina was excited I had found a new approach
and we immediately started to actively prepare the film.
It took more than a year of learning and testing
to understand and overcome the initial inadequacies of the new language.
After all, these were still the childhood days of 3D.
When we were finally ready, in the summer of 2009,
it turned out we were too late.
Pina Bausch died of cancer on 30 June, abruptly and unexpectedly.
That was the end of a common dream that had lasted twenty years.

Without Pina, none of what we had planned was possible any more.
In a tragic way, it seemed,
we had hesitated for too long to make this film,
or rather: had waited for 3D for too long.
(Then again, to soothe my regrets and my pains,
we could not have done it any sooner.)
I gave up on the project and pulled the plug.

The fact that the film was made after all
is strictly due to the dancers of the Tanztheater.
They did not give up,
but decided to continue and to fulfil all the obligations
that the company had undertaken with Pina.

They even performed on the night when they learned about Pina's death,
playing in tears,
knowing that was what Pina would have wanted them to do.
She meant it when she said:
'Dance, dance, otherwise, we are lost!'

So, weeks later, they also started rehearsing the pieces
that Pina had put on the agenda for our film.
And that was the turning point:
these four pieces that Pina had wanted so much to be filmed
and to be preserved in that new language
were going to be played, anyway,
and maybe for the last time!
Cancelling the film had been the wrong reaction,
it slowly dawned on me.
We could no longer do the film *with* Pina that we had planned.
But together we could do a film *for* Pina!
It would be an homage to her,
but also a way for all of us to say goodbye, and thanks,
to deal with the loss and the grief,
and to come to terms with Pina's death.

So from one day to another we jump-started the film.
And we were ready just in time to shoot the four pieces.
We did not know yet what else to do.
These plays on their own would not constitute a film – far from it.
But there was no concept yet
to replace everything we had planned to do together with Pina,
with her in front of the camera *and* behind.
The film that needed to be done
would now have to be invented on the spot.

When the pieces were recorded,
we interrupted the shoot for several months.
We had no clue how to continue.
I started editing,
curious about how the material that we shot so far would cut.
And hoping that it would somehow reveal a continuation.

~

We had preserved Pina's pieces, like she had wanted, in their entirety.
How could I still approach *my* angle, to film *her eyes at work*,
now she was no longer with us?
In the editing room it hit me one day:
Pina's look had rested on these dancers for years and years,
day in and day out...
They could tell me!
And not in interviews!
This was going to be a film without interviews, I had promised Pina.
All I had to do was employ Pina's own method,
the way she had developed all her pieces!
I would ask the dancers about the nature of Pina's look,
what she saw in them that they were not even aware of,
how she always saw the best in them,
when they felt closer to her than ever before, or after, etc....
and, just like in the routine with Pina,
they would not be allowed to answer questions with words
but in their own language: dancing.
I proposed that to them and they all agreed.

Each and every one of them eventually showed me their answers.
Those were not improvisations; I had made that a condition.
(After all, I was not a choreographer
and was in no position to judge improvisations.)
It was all material they had worked on with Pina,
that Pina's eyes had been on,
and that had been used in previous pieces,
or had been eliminated in the editing process for a piece.

For these 'danced answers'
we did not have a stage any more, let alone sets.
So I decided to take the dancers outside,
into the city and the adjoining industrial landscape.
I looked for a specific place for each and every one
that could bring out the best in each answer.
Of course I did not interfere with the choreographic part of it.
But I could now show the dances from all sides
and could have my camera dance along with them.
Those exterior shots became the bulk of the film.

The dancers and I, we worked together, over a period of almost one year,
in several instalments.

Toward the end of the shoot, almost as an afterthought,
we shot with each and every one of the dancers
what we called our 'silent portraits'.
They consisted of a medium-size close-up of each dancer,
just sitting in front of the camera.
There were no words, no sound recording,
and my only indication was:
'You are on your own, all alone, just resting in yourself,
and after a while, on your very own timing,
you will find a way to look into the camera, as if it was a friend,
somebody very close, whom you are certainly not afraid of.'

We did these portraits in a corner of the Opera's exercise room.
They turned out to become the most exciting thing
of our one-year-long 3D experience!
Not our complicated dance shots were the revelation
– some of them choreographed in complex ways,
with hundreds of crane and camera moves for takes as long as one hour –
no, the most exciting experience was the most simple one: close-ups.
There is nothing more ordinary in filmmaking.

For these portraits I sent the whole crew away,
so I was just alone with each dancer,
sitting behind the camera,
looking at the little 3D control monitor on my lap.
And *that* was unbelievable!
It surpassed everything I had expected from 3D.
I had dreamed, of course, of dance to be shown adequately,
and as naturally as possible,
and 'space' and 'depth' had been the ways to achieve that,
but all of a sudden,
something else emerged in front of these two eyes of our camera:
There was a *person* in front of the camera, and in front of me
(eventually also in front of the audience!).
A real *body*!
Not just a shape, a cut-out figure,
like in a hundred years of cinema before.

There was '*volume*'!
Roundness!
Shoulders were sculptures.
A face was a landscape,

no longer a flat surface,
like in any close-up I had ever seen before!
There was a true 'presence' to each and every body!
It had *the aura* that you can only feel
when you are confronting somebody
and really *recognise* him, or her,
when you can reach out and *touch*,
not only with your hands.
You can also touch somebody with your eyes,
when he (or she) is there,
with you and in front of you.
When there is a *you* and a *me*,
myself and *the other* ...

That is a situation we only know from life, not from cinema.
In movies, the screen itself, the flatness of it,
creates an abstraction.
I am always *here*, sitting *here* on my chair in the movie theatre,
inside me, inside my reality,
and whoever is on the screen is apart from that,
even if the story creates the strongest identification.
We know that.
We have *space* around us.
That is what our perception needs in order to give us a sense of reality.
The flat screen only has an illusory fake space,
an emotional space (in a good movie)
that we can immerse in for two hours, sure,
but it is essentially the same space a painting has, or a photograph.
Until now those were definitely separate
from the reality of our own space.

When I sat in front of these actors/dancers
just a couple of metres away, behind the camera,
alone in the room with them,
I was still talking to them, they looked at me,
I gave them some last direction,
we shared the space of the I AND YOU,
and then I stopped talking and left them on their own
and looked at the little monitor,
that I was holding, after all, in my hands,
like I had been holding lots of computers or iPads or screens.

which future of seeing?

I realised with an immense shock
that some of the mystery, the intimacy,
the uniqueness of a human encounter
that we *never ever* granted the movie screen to possess
or to be able to carry and capture . . .
that some of that *was* indeed there, in this three-dimensional image!
I must say: I was unprepared.
We had been using this technology for weeks already,
and had started to 'understand' it,
learn how to move the camera,
learn how to deal with 'depth' and 'space',
but this sheer presence of a person,
without a choreography, without sound, without story,
almost without purpose,
was . . . mind-boggling.

I had not seen that in any film before,
neither in any previous 3D film, that's for sure,
nor in our own footage.
How this medium was able to actually transcend
(in the very sense of the word)
the realm of cinema, of cinematic representation,
and create (or imitate, I'm not sure) 'presence',
human presence, in body and soul . . .
that was shocking.
What possibilities opened up all of a sudden
for stories and documentaries to use that intimacy,
and to share that common space of 'being there' . . .
I was overwhelmed with the prospect of a whole different kind of cinema
that would immerse us and involve us!
We could be taken into somebody else's world like never before!

The most outrageous, though, was, or *is*:
the present perception of 3D is going in the opposite direction.
It is all taking place in the realm of fantasy,
and the actors on the screen are more devoid of reality
than any actor in an old black and white movie.
And that goes for everything
that comes packaged in the 3D envelope of the Major Studios, so far.
They have taken this language, this amazing new medium, and . . .
kidnapped it, stolen it, mutilated it beyond recognition,
so none of their audiences could possibly conceive of it

as a tool to represent ... *reality*.
Human reality. Our planet. Our existence. Our concerns.
But: I am convinced that this is what 3D was invented for
and what it can do.

Remember: when digital technology came up in movies,
in the early to mid-Nineties, it first appeared in commercials,
very expensive video clips
(we all learned the word 'morphing' from a Michael Jackson video)
and in expensive special effect shots to basically blow up the entire world.
Remember: when we all watched 9/11
most of us first thought it looked like movie scenes we had seen before.
The word 'digital' had a strange smell.
It smelled of 'manipulating', 'cheating',
messing with reality and with the truth.
But only a few years later
'digital cinema' appeared to us under a very different aspect:
digital technology single-handedly saved the documentary form
and even single-handedly reinvented it.
The documentary had been practically dead at that point,
expelled from movie theatres for more than a decade already.
We owe the fact that there are hundreds
of good and important documentaries every year
strictly to these (once scary) digital tools.

The very same thing is happening with 3D.
It got out of bed on the wrong foot.
People think it is strictly a fantasy tool owned by the Big Studios.
And the studios have no interest whatsoever in proving the opposite.
They have no interest in developing 3D as a 'language'.
As long as it rakes in the money,
they are happy not to explore it in any other way
than as an attraction in itself.
But 3D can do/can be so much more!
It deserves to be taken seriously!
It should/it will/it must
become the very language of future reality-based movies,
documentaries as well as fictional films.
It is absurd that the contemporary notion of a 'fictional film' means,
for more and more people today,
that it is *not* related to any reality.
That is a cultural disaster, a tsunami wiping out our imagination.

Stories are rooted in myth,
and myth is distilled from human experience, from life.
Stories are not recycled versions of other stories
that are already formulated from previous stories.
(Which is the present state of the blockbuster cinema.
But I am getting carried away ...)

3D has a totally unexplored affinity to the reality of the human presence.
I had stumbled upon this, by sheer luck, so to speak.
It had been possible because Alain Derobe, my stereographer,
had put these (mostly prototype) tools into our hands,
because these amazing people, Pina's dancers,
had been willing to share this work of grief with us,
and because they had been prepared,
through the years of working with Pina,
to let go of any role-playing, to act any 'parts',
and just be themselves, as much as possible,
on stage just as well as in front of a camera.
3D belongs in the hands of documentary filmmakers,
of independent writers, directors, authors,
of people willing and able to forget limits, rules, formulas, recipes,
and enter a whole new age of cinema,
where there is more ... *connexion*.
Existential connection.
3D has that connecting power ...

Of course, the presence of a human being, even amazingly enhanced by 3D,
is still a virtual one, like in the old cinema.
And nothing will ever replace the real encounter, person to person.
But look at our situation:
in the age of ever more images circulating the globe with increasing speed,
we *look* at them, numbly,
but we don't have the time and the skills any more to *see*,
let alone to feel empathy,
or even reflect upon the loss in the act of seeing.
In terms of imagery, few things can still touch us.
3D, in my book, can help renew that capacity
and restore our susceptibility to be concerned by an image.
(After all, three-dimensional perception
occupies different areas of our brains.)

Now you will frown and think of me as an incurable optimist.
Maybe I am,
but I think stories and documentaries in 3D
could actually make us *see* differently again
and respond to pictures in a more involved way.
Potentially, that is. (I know.)
It could very well happen,
that the new language is already abused by sensationalism
and we're the victims of another overkill.

~

During that year we were shooting *Pina*,
Avatar came out, on Christmas of 2009.
I thought it was a masterpiece,
a grand vision like they happen only too rarely in the history of cinema.
When I saw the film for the first time,
I was very excited over two thirds into it.
I was certain: these peaceful people on that distant planet, the Na'vi,
would be able to do something unexpected, utopian,
in their fight to defend their place and their culture.
They were totally non-violent, had no concept of war,
and they would find a way to deal with the aggressor
in a surprising and peaceful way.
How disappointed was I to see that in its last third
the film turned into yet another war movie, after all.
It had so many (dramaturgic) chances to take another route
that would have lifted it up to a glorious metaphor.
But no, it didn't.
Here it was again,
that American glorification of war,
overpowering and victorious
(even in movies of the best intention).
Aren't almost all major successes in film history
based on violence and war?
Star Wars even carries that paradigm in its title.
War rules, even out there, in the universe.

The world that Cameron had created was amazing,
and I loved the film for its grand scale of invention.
But on the other hand it showed painfully
that a new language (with all its potential)

was already firmly in the grip of an old language
in which violence and war always persevere and take the upper hand.
It would have been so easy
(and so close that I had actually been expecting it)
to establish a new rule.
Wishful thinking,
considering we're dealing with an industry driven by profit margins ...

In the movies that followed *Avatar* over the next few years, however,
the possibilities of 3D got hopelessly lost.
The new language was only used for effects, not for changing perception.
I found myself stumbling out of one mindless waste of time after another.

Still, my deepest desire, or biggest hope
is that this future 3D cinema
will in fact ignite a new interest in *the act of seeing*,
in the *physiology* and *psychology*
of what our eyes and our brains do together, in unison,
in the most amazing perfection,
to *create* space, depth, volume and presence.
Every day, right now, 'in life',
when you put down this book and go outside,
when you see the world, your friends, or kids, or neighbours,
your eyes and your spatial perception are miracles!

That is what 3D tries to imitate and could *become*:
a miraculously new/old way to perceive life,
in which we are more immersed and concerned again.
There is still a long way to go;
this is an adventurous road
into a territory that is still largely unexplored, cinematically,
yet so well known, humanly and physiologically.
I look at it as a chance,
but it might very well be
that the new language is wasted before it can fulfil its promises.

future of seeing

What the film *Pina* does is establish a world of relation: the new connection between the human body and technology enhances and extends visual and cinematic language. Crossing the boundaries of dance and the cinematic image, the camera that *dances* with us demonstrates the grace and beauty of the human body and its unique language. This is an experience that can move beyond the 'certificate of presence' that we spoke of earlier into a different kind of presence, space and beauty. This method of looking may resonate with Weil's notion of the beautiful:

> The attitude of looking and waiting is the attitude which corresponds with the beautiful. As long as one can go on conceiving, wishing, longing, the beautiful does not appear. That is why in all beauty we find contradiction, bitterness and absence which are irreducible.[30]

We have explored throughout this chapter how to discern the virtues and sensibilities of peace in a technological age – that is, extending a visual and moral language that can transform how we see. Ultimately, the future of seeing relies on past virtues reinvented in new and unforeseen ways. Rainer Maria Rilke's poem 'Archaic Torso of Apollo' reminds us of this hope and beauty:

> We never knew his head and all the light
> that ripened in his fabled eyes. But
> his torso still burns like a streetlamp dimmed
> in which his gaze, lit long ago,
>
> holds fast and shines. Otherwise the surge
> of the breast could not blind you so, nor a smile
> run through the slight twist of the loins
> toward that center where procreation flared.
>
> Otherwise this stone would stand cut off
> and cold under the shoulders' transparent drop
> and not glisten like a wild beast's fur;
>
> and not break forth from all its contours
> like a star: for there is no place
> that does not see you. You must change your life.
>
> *Wir kannten nicht sein unerhörtes*
> *Haupt, darin die Augenäpfel reiften. Aber*
> *sein Torso glüht noch wie ein Kandelaber,*
> *in dem sein Schauen, nur zurückgeschraubt,*

> sich hält und glänzt. Sonst könnte nicht der Bug
> der Brust dich blenden, und im leisen Drehen
> der Lenden könnte nicht ein Lächeln gehen
> zu jener Mitte, die die Zeugung trug.
>
> Sonst stünde dieser Stein entstellt und kurz
> unter der Schultern durchsichtigem Sturz
> und flimmerte nicht so wie Raubtierfelle;
>
> und bräche nicht aus allen seinen Rändern
> aus wie ein Stern: denn da ist keine Stelle,
> die dich nicht sieht. Du musst dein Leben ändern.[31]

Joshua Tree Military Lights
(Wim Wenders)

A Postcard from Joshua Tree

An important part of our common effort
to write this book together, Mary and me,
took place in a remote cabin near Joshua Tree
in the Mojave desert in California.
It was getting to be winter,
and the days became quite short.
We started our work with sunrise to make the most of daylight.
At night we could only work at candlelight.

Our cabin was situated in the foothills,
and we had a huge vista in front of us.
From the window facing north
we overlooked a valley of rocks and desert shrub
behind which rose a low ridge of mountains.
At the rear of those hills spread another huge valley,
 a real sandy desert,
with yet another higher mountain ridge at the horizon.
And in front of those mountains, in the far distance,
a navy base was situated.
At night the military compound glistened in the distance
like a phantom city,
or like an invasion from another planet.
Every now and then we heard detonations, also at night.
And once, in the middle of the day,
a grey mushroom cloud stood over that whole area.

Working on wrapping our thoughts around the notion of peace,
it felt like our 'opponents' were always looming at the horizon,
ready to demonstrate their power,

while in the foreground
all sorts of birds, squirrels, chipmunks, rabbits and lizards
were having the best of times.

Looking at these animals, a thought came to my mind:
Peace is.
War wants to be.

*

In these last days of writing, I walk along the desert road in a beautiful dawn light. This road is part of the Mojave desert, ancient in its feel and location. In this beautiful light, I stop to take some photos.

The desert gives a strange sense of solitude and beauty. You can almost feel the dawning of the gods that comes out of such ecology; the great religions all stem from this common source and landscape. In its starkness, the desert is teeming with life other than our own. There is something mystical here.

Buried among what appear as hostile plants and terrain are the most exquisite creatures; the landscape has this sense of peace that we have been writing about, the elements which constitute a spiritual and physical unity. The oldest living plants live in the desert, too, the creosote bush with its unique smell after the rains. Birds come and go; they are not frightened by human shadows and shadows of the earth. They live by the desert and its winds. As I continue to walk along the road, I am endlessly awestruck by the desert.

Again I stop. This time I am aware of the silence; it is so quiet here. When I stop I can hear and feel my own heartbeat. My body is pulsating, or at least that is what I think. I feel deeply satisfied at this moment, some kind of spiritual awakening...

After a while, I decide it is time to start walking again. Slowly I come to realise that the 'beat' that I hear is no longer coming from inside of my body, but the pulse seems to be coming from outside of it. It feels sort of strange. I'm somewhat perplexed; but it seems to me that the desert must bring about these strange awakenings...

Later that morning, the local caretaker drives by our cabin to check if Wim and I need any supplies. He points out the naval base that is thirty miles in the distance and tells us that they regularly detonate bombs there. This morning was no exception. He comments that every time he sees a bomb flare on the horizon or feels its effects, he thinks another ten thousand dollars have gone to waste.

a postcard from joshua tree

I began to realise that my bodily pulsation and 'heartbeat' I had experienced earlier was part of a morning ritual, the detonating of bombs in this remote desert region. Our bodies become intimate vessels of war; we can confuse the moments of beauty with moments of destruction, as we become aligned or habituated to certain artificial beats and reverberations.

This experience was sobering.

*

The 'natural world' invites us to share with it; the land speaks, it does not detonate. In this sense the world is given to us as a gift. In this shared world in all its shapes and forms lies a deeper connection to the unity of time and sense of place, as well to life and its mystery.

Now, as I write this, I remember the gift of all that surrounds me. Even in the wake of a bomb there is the memory of peace that is already here, ancient as well as present, a kind of exaltation that surrounds even as it harbours the chaos of the human world and its turmoil. It offers us its beauty. 'Yes', it seems, is the holy word here, since to affirm and to create is the only way to inspire hope and peace. And it is from this state of joy that we can learn how to dream again.

To say farewell then to this place of writing, there can be no conclusion, only a question to keep considering: how to invent peace each in our own way as well as *all* together. And to give thanks for the sphere that exists between *You and I*, to be grateful for this world in which we might believe in it again, where we can live with a certain awareness for the world and others; this awareness brings me great solace and hope for all that is, and is to come.

Postscript – Do Men Fuck it Up?!

When Joseph Conrad wrote The Heart of Darkness,
he was referring to his experiences for a Belgian shipping company
for whom he had worked as a captain of a steamer
that was running up and down the Congo River.
He was then stationed in a little town named Kabalo,
midway down the river.
Kabalo was once an industrious town,
when the cotton industry in the area was prosperous.

There are no more boats going down the river today.
You see a few carcasses of them here and there
rotting away in the mud along the shores.

The train station of Kabalo was once a busy hub,
with trains leaving east and west, north and south.
Now a handful of run-down engines serve an area as big as Central Europe
and it might take weeks to get from Kabalo to Lubumbashi,
depending which erratic schedule the train might be following.
All streets leading to Kabalo are destroyed and eaten up again by the bush.

Countless years of civil wars, rebel violence and tribal conflicts
have devastated Kabalo.
There is no more electricity, no more running water,
no more jobs, no more industry.
Still, some thirty thousand people live here,
in the remnants of houses, in self-made huts,
in streets that still have lamp posts,
but that disappear every night in total darkness.
Kabalo, more than Joseph Conrad ever envisioned,

is the heart of darkness today.

I was there for three weeks in the summer of 2006.
I arrived with the supply plane of 'Doctors Without Borders'
that lands on the dirt strip near the town.
Yes, there once was an airport.
The leftovers of the cement tower are a witness to that.
But the pilot has to find his own way down today,
nobody is helping or guiding him.

Still, a few soldiers wait for us, when the plane comes to a stop.
We are warned that we should not film or take any pictures.
The 'airport' is a 'military installation', even if the only 'building' in use
consists of nothing but a small tin roof over four sticks
to shield the soldiers from the blazing sun.
So we keep our equipment in their boxes,
and I just take a couple of hidden snapshots with my mobile phone.
It's of no use here for anything else, anyway.
There doesn't seem to be any reception.

'We' are my Swiss cameraman, Alberto,
my American sound engineer, Andrew, and myself.
We are the crew of a documentary film
we want to shoot in Kabalo for Doctors Without Borders.
Actually, for the Spanish faction of the doctors.
They are going to have their twentieth anniversary next year,
and for that occasion thought of a movie.
No, not about themselves – the doctors are not vain.
They wanted to have a film dealing with their work.
Every year they establish a list of what they call 'The Invisibles',
Ten diseases or conflicts that the world does not pay enough attention to.
They asked Spanish actor Javier Bardem to executive-produce that film,
who in turn asked a handful of film directors
if they wanted to participate in the project,
and each chose one of the 'invisible diseases' from the list.
Mariano Barroso, Isabel Coixet, Javier Corcuera
and Fernando León de Aranoa
were my fellow directors,
all of us shooting in different countries.

The morning after our arrival in Kabalo
I find myself explaining my subject to the military authorities.

postscript – do men fuck it up?!

They have to grant a permit to the foreigners
so they're allowed to stay in Kabalo for three weeks.
The doctors advise me to be very frank about our purpose.
'They'll find out anyway, so better be honest about it.'
We wait in one of the few brick buildings, in an empty waiting room,
and half an hour later stand in front of the military governor.
He sits behind an empty desk that only carries an old telephone
that we know cannot be working.
We are a film crew, I explain,
we are staying at the hospital of Doctors Without Borders,
and we plan to be here for three weeks.
We intend to make a short film about violence against women.

The man listens to my French, nods,
looks at the chief administrator of the hospital who accompanies us,
and when he nods his confirmation, the officer turns back to me.
Of course we are welcome to stay, he says,
subject to his approval and to an administrative fee.
Again he looks at our local representative.
He nods again. He knows and already prepared us,
that we'll have to pay for these 'visitor's permits'.
It's a bribe, that is obvious.
It'll be the most expensive factor in our otherwise low budget.

What else would we have to know?
The man explains it to us.
We are not allowed, under any circumstances,
to film military installations, buildings, or personnel.
Whenever we see a soldier, or policeman,
we have to immediately stop shooting,
otherwise our tapes and our equipment will be confiscated.
We agree, but have to leave our passports and our visa.
Again, we sit for a long time in the waiting room,
before we get our passports back,
now adorned by an additional stamp on top of our Congolese permits,
stating that we are allowed to remain in Kabalo for three weeks.
Every man in town is soon going to know what we're here for …

We will try to make a film on a subject
that ranks high on the doctors' sad list:
'Violence against women' is indeed a disease
that they are taking more and more seriously.

They have started to train doctors and nurses to be equipped to confront it
and help women who have become victims of rape.
Systematic raping has become, indeed,
a more and more frequent means of any warfare,
in many areas of conflict all over the world.

Initially, we had intended to shoot in Darfur
and planned our journey there together with the organisation.
But then Doctors Without Borders were forced to leave the area,
as their security could no longer be assured, let alone ours.
So they had to look for another place for us to shoot,
where it was just as relevant to deal with the subject.
Kabalo came up,
because the doctors operate a hospital here for some time already,
and the ongoing conflicts with rebel troops such as the Mai-Mai
had led to a disastrously high number of women
who had become victims of systematic rape.

My cameraman and I live in a windowless room of eight square metres
in the guest house of the hospital where most of the doctors reside.
The hospital has a generator
that we can plug into every night for a couple of hours
to charge our cameras, computers and other batteries.
There is a German 'logistics manager',
but all the nurses and doctors are Spanish.
We see them occasionally in the morning or the evening
when we eat together.
All our Spanish doctors are chain-smokers,
and the most wanted goods on the weekly plane
are the cigarette supplies.

We start preparing our film.
There is a key instructor from the head office of Doctors Without Borders
with us in Kabalo,
and she has already established a contact with a local self-help group.
These are women who, without any funding or outside help,
try to assist women and girls who have become victims of rape.
They have a list of more than four hundred women in this area
whom they have helped and whom they are in contact with.
They will talk to some of the women whose stories they know
and find out who'd be willing to talk to us.

postscript – do men fuck it up?!

In the meantime
my team and I explore the area in and around Kabalo a bit.
A huge crowd of people has just arrived at the train station,
several hundreds of them, with many children among them.
They had to get off the train and are now stranded,
as the train conductor decided (against better payment, I suppose)
to change the schedule and drive east instead of north to Lubumbashi,
formerly Elisabethville.
These people will be here for days, possibly weeks,
all camping on the ground around the station.
The doctors are worried about sanitation
and immediately send a delegation to the site.
We go with them.

The camp looks like a disaster zone.
There are indeed hundreds of people sitting between the train tracks,
some with fires, some preparing make-shift tents.
Many children running around, mostly naked.
There is a station manager.
He lives with his family on the spacious first floor of the building.
He has locked up the ground floor of the station,
so none of these people can get inside.
Which means they have no access to the toilets in the waiting room.
Yes, there are indeed eight toilets!
The doctors visit them and explain to the station manager
that without the use of these toilets it will be just a matter of days
before there's going to be an outbreak of cholera
among the crowd outside.

The man demands money.
He'll only open these toilets if the doctors will pay for it.
They can't and they won't: if they gave in to such blackmail,
they could give up on their entire work right away, they explain to us.
Flying in toilets would take way too long.
The doctors feel helpless ...
The only thing to do is get ready to fight the outbreak of cholera
and disinfect the areas around the station
that will have to make up for the missing toilets.
We film some of the chaos around the station.
Soldiers arrive and we have to stop shooting.
There is a flag pole by the station,
and at sunset the soldiers bring down the Congolese flag ...

The next day we drive around and visit adjoining villages.
As we are in a jeep with the sign of Doctors Without Borders on it,
we are greeted friendly and welcome everywhere.
As the doctors treat everybody, friends or enemies, soldiers or rebels,
they are widely respected.
They advise us to wear the vests with their logo at all times.
It makes us feel very protected, indeed.

We do not see many men.
Do they know why we're here and do they avoid contact with us?
They're just not around ...
In the morning, and in the late afternoon,
I do see some young men playing basketball or soccer.
Every now and then a motorbike drives by,
and those would only be owned by men.
Also the bicycles only have male riders.
All the work on the fields is done by women.
All the water is brought from the wells or from the river by women.
All the work around the houses is done by women.
All the work on the market, all the shopping, buying and selling.
I see a young guy repairing bikes.
He seems to be the only working man around ...
What are the men doing?
There is enough to be done, in the fields and in the town,
enough damage to be repaired, enough land lying wasted.
No, there are no jobs, I am told.
The only paid jobs, basically, are as soldiers or policemen.

We visit the school.
Here, some of the teachers are men, at least,
but most of them are women, too.
The headmaster is walking around with a stick.
We see him beat children with his stick, for no apparent reason.

As we are looking for locations
to shoot our future interviews with the women,
we soon realise this is a difficult task.
There are no public buildings that we could use,
all the houses that remained intact are owned by the military.
To shoot in nature is rather impossible.
As soon as we get out of the car anywhere,
we are surrounded by hundreds of children.

postscript – do men fuck it up?!

We'd want the women we will be talking to,
– and we still have to find them –
to feel safe and protected.
What they might tell us will not be for any other ears …

The huts of the local people are all windowless.
It is too dark inside to consider shooting in there.
There is no electricity, and we have no lights with us, anyway.
And you would hear any word from outside …
After a few days we realise that the classrooms of the school,
– once school is over in the afternoon –
are the only protected and relatively intimate places
where we could conduct our interviews.
The roofs are open, all caved in, so we can shoot with available light.
The women of the self-help association come with the first stories.
They first need to be translated from Swahili
and two other local languages into French.
Finally, we have a collection of about a dozen accounts by women
who would also be willing to tell these stories in front of a camera.

We read them all carefully and select six of them.
Then we meet with these six women and explain to them,
with the help and the interpretation by the ladies of the association,
what the movie is about and what we would want from them.
They all agree to do these interviews,
as long as they can be done in an intimate and secure setting.
Two of the women are still very young, under sixteen,
and on a suggestion of the women's association
we plan to film them in a way that their faces cannot be recognised.

In the meantime, we have been joined by an additional team member,
a Senegalese camera assistant, Fatoumata Kande.
She flew in from Dakar, but had to go via Amsterdam to
make it to the Democratic Republic of Congo.
We realised that it would be difficult for our interviews
if the women were facing only us, three white men.
Fatou will operate the first camera,
so that the women will confront a black woman, most of all.
Alberto will operate the second camera from the side,
and Andrew and myself will keep at a distance
with the headphones and the sound recording device.

The ladies of the association block the area around the school buildings,
so that nobody can come to the classrooms,
and we can indeed be totally undisturbed.
We dedicate one afternoon to each of the women.

From the start it becomes obvious that the questions we have prepared
(and which the interpreter has in front of her)
are more or less obsolete.
As we have explained to the women
what we want them to tell into our camera,
they all start on their own, as soon as the camera is rolling,
and they all talk more or less without interruption, until their story is told.

I do not understand what they say.
It seems out of the question to interrupt them,
in order to have a translation.
Sometimes there are longer pauses,
which the women need to gather themselves,
but they all go on with their accounts without being asked.
So we shoot until each of them has finished talking.
The interpreter then turns toward us and indicates
that all subjects of our questionnaire have been covered.

The women give their accounts in a very matter-of-fact way,
amazingly unemotional,
punctuated by sharp little cries or shouts,
some clapping of the hands,
and by many gestures, shrugs and waves.
One of them wants to tell her story together with her husband.
They went through their ordeal together,
and have stuck to each other afterwards.
Many of the women, we are told,
are left by their husbands after being raped.
Only when we hear the first translation, word by word,
in the evening at the hospital,
we are shocked and deeply moved by each story,
the honesty of the account and the lack of self-pity.

We continue like this for a week,
listening to the tapes at night, often in tears.
It takes time to establish a good translation,
because the local languages give room for a lot of interpretation,

postscript – do men fuck it up?!

and we want to find out as exactly as possible
what the women meant to say.
Later, in the editing room in Berlin,
it will be much harder to ask for explanations ...

When we finish our interviews,
we continue to shoot for a couple of days,
mainly with the women of the association,
to give us an overview of the situation and to explain their work to us.
They speak in a mixture of Swahili and French.
As we want to film them all together,
we find one room in a nearby village
that serves as community room and church,
and the stage is wide enough for the ladies to
sit together on benches, in two rows.

These women are quite tough and have seen all sorts of hardship.
Still, they are overwhelmed a few times
by the sheer amount of violence and suffering
that they are exposed to on a daily level.
We also find out how the work of the association started:
the eldest of them, and one of the two leaders,
had lost her daughter, who was kidnapped by the Mai-Mai,
and she was never able to find her again.
At the end of the long session, the ladies start singing a song,
tentatively at first and then with more and more confidence.
They have written it themselves; it is their hymn to female solidarity.
My entire little crew stands there weeping.

Then we are finished with our task.
We have a few days left,
before the supply plane from Lubumbashi passes Kabalo again.
Early one morning we hear train whistling,
a lot of shouting and commotion,
and when we run to the station with our camera
we can only film the last wagons of the train crossing the road,
with hundreds of people in and on them,
waving from the windows and the roofs.
They are happy to finally leave Kabalo again.
As predicted, there *was* a cholera epidemic at the station,
with several deaths,
and the hospital is overflowing with patients,

now all left behind, and some abandoned by their families.
Who knows when they can catch another train north?

We spend some time shooting in the market and in the streets of Kabalo.
That's how we find out where a lot of the men are during the days.
They are at 'the cinema'!
That's a euphemism
for a half fallen-down house at the main junction of Kabalo.
An Indian businessman installed a noisy little generator here,
providing enough power to run a DVD player and a crummy TV set.
Four or five films are on his chalk-board agenda every day,
from early in the afternoon to late at night.
Some action and karate films, but most of all war movies.
They make the bulk of his programming.
These are certainly all bootlegged copies, of a lousy quality,
but that doesn't do any harm to the success of this business.
The 'theatre' is always full, and crammed at night.

The audience is strictly, and a hundred per cent, men.
Older men, young men, and kids, too.
For some of them the films are way too cruel and violent,
but nobody seems to care.
The entire audience sits in silence and stares at the TV monitor
that depicts war scenes and fighting practically all day long.

These men, and especially the children, know nothing but war, anyway.
The history of the country, after the horrors of the Belgian colonisation,
was one never-ending civil war of fifty years,
and armed conflicts are still going on in the area,
even if this is the first year of peace.
There are the first 'free elections' coming up soon,
which we only know too well,
because there are posters everywhere,
and every morning, at the break of dawn,
men with bullhorns roam the streets,
blaring slogans and empty promises at the citizens of Kabalo,
just as they wake up.
Sometimes they have real shouting matches,
like 'walking propaganda radios',
and their voices are distorted and shrieking in such a way
that I assume nobody can actually understand their messages any more.

postscript – do men fuck it up?!

What are the programmes of all these political parties?
I ask one of the doctors' local staff one day,
the only man who speaks good French
and who had an education by Catholic sisters,
probably before the independence.
He does not understand my question. A programme?
Yes, what do they stand for? ...
For themselves only, he explains, their only 'programme' is to be elected.
'Vote for me!' is the political message of all of them...

My crew and I decide to make a short film centred on the cinema,
and on the men's addiction to war that is so sadly apparent there.
No problem to get 'permission' – that only costs a bit of money.
The problem is rather that the cinema is too dark, especially in the evening.
There is no other light source than the TV screen.
Our professional cameras can't handle these conditions,
but my consumer equipment has a feature called 'night shot'.
It films with an inbuilt infra-red light,
so we can shoot in total darkness.

We start in the afternoon,
on the street corner where the 'cinema' is located.
One speaker blares the sound of the film that is running
out over the entire square.
Then we continue filming inside.
Black Hawk Down is the movie,
a film about the failed American mission in Somalia.
There is a lot of shooting and helicopter action.
None of the men, and certainly none of the children, take notice of us.
They all watch, transfixed.
Much of the sound in the 'theatre' comes from the generator next door,
and then, of course, from the film itself, over the crummy speakers.
Gunshots, tanks, helicopters, soldiers shouting commands ...
The film is dubbed into French.

Staring on the little control monitor of my camera
I see the faces of the children
that are just a couple of metres in front of me, in the dark.
They are terrified and utterly scared,
but can't turn their eyes away from the screen.

When we walk out again, the sun has already set,

and in the twilight a military band passes, with drums and flutes
(what is this, a recruiting operation?),
and a dozen kids follow them, like the Pied Piper.

The next day we leave Kabalo.
In Lubumbashi, we have another stop for a couple of days,
before we can catch a flight to Nairobi.
Again, we stay at the local headquarters of Doctors Without Borders.
There is one big hotel in Lubumbashi,
but it is exclusively for Chinese guests.
Other people can't even get near it.
I see a lot of construction sites in the city, especially road building.
All of these seem to be financed and controlled by Chinese companies.
Also, when we're finally leaving,
the 'VIP lounge' at the airport is not for business passengers, as I find out.
It rather specifies on the sign underneath: 'For Chinese passengers only'.
In the airplane, apart from my little crew and myself
there are mostly Chinese and a few African passengers.
I feel totally numb when I look down on the African landscape
as the plane makes its way east towards Kenya.
I can't help the sinking feeling that this continent will not get better,
unless women can play a decisive role in curing it.
Most of the men I met were hopeless.
Corrupt, selfish, lazy, lying and irresponsible.
The women were carrying all the weight,
but without getting any recognition for it whatsoever.
On the contrary, they were treated as non-people, non-existent, invisible.
I feel a deep anger rising in me against my own gender.
There are no wars started by women.
There is no violence or killing initiated by women.
There is little exploitation or abuse conducted by women...

I look down on the vast expanses
and actually find myself thinking and then writing into my notebook:
'They should just send all the men on a long holiday
and let women run the continent for a while!'
Africa, probably the world itself, would be a better place.

As we pass Mount Kilimanjaro,
the captain points out to his Chinese, African and European passengers,
– all of them men, without a single exception! –
that it is the first time in his life

postscript – do men fuck it up?!

that he sees the big mountain without any snow cap on top.

The Chinese don't even look out.
The Africans look out and some of them notice.
I stare at the majestic mountain and start crying.
All the pressure and the impressions of these last weeks burst out at once.
Yes, men fuck it up big time!

The two short films *Invisible Crimes* and *War in Peace* can be seen on our website: www.inventing-peace.com – the access code for *Invisible Crimes* is IBT-CRIMES, the access code for *War in Peace* is IBT-PEACE.

Notes

Prelude
1 See Mary Zournazi, *Hope – New Philosophies for Change* (New York: Routledge, 2003).
2 George Lakoff wrote a very lucid book on language and morality as well as how good versus evil framed public debate in the aftermath of 9/11. See George Lakoff, *Don't Think of an Elephant: Know Your Values and Frame the Debate* (Melbourne: Scribe, 2005).
3 Throughout the book we often cite the original English spelling of 'connexion'. Etymologically speaking, connexion in its historical use has a closer link to the idea of the spirit and sacredness. We use 'connexion' when it speaks more closely to this spiritual connection, and in other cases we refer to 'connection' in its more usual spelling and usage.
4 Rilke's *Duino Elegies* were first published in 1923. See Rainer Maria Rilke, *The Poetry of Rilke*, ed. and trans. Edward Snow (New York: North Point Press, 2009), pp. 282–3.
5 Rudolf Otto, *The Idea of the Holy*, trans. John W. Harvey (Oxford: Oxford University Press, 1958), p. 135.
6 Aldous Huxley, *The Perennial Philosophy* (London: Chatto & Windus, 1957), pp. 222–3.
7 Maurice Merleau-Ponty, *The Visible and Invisible*, trans. Alphonso Lingis (Evanston, IL: Northwestern University Press), p. 196.
8 See Michelangelo Antonioni's *The Architecture of Vision*, ed. Marga Cottino-Jones (New York: Marisilio Publishers, 1996).
9 Émile Durkheim, *The Elementary Forms of Religious Life*, trans. Carol Cosman (Oxford: Oxford University Press, 2001), pp. 317–18.
10 See Michel Serres, *Angels: A Modern Myth*, trans. Francis Cowper and ed. Philippa Hurd (Paris and New York: Flammarion, 1995).
11 Serres, *Angels*, inside cover.
12 Philosopher Georges Bataille might call this a 'sacred sociology'. See Georges Bataille and Roger Caillois, 'Sacred Sociology and the Relationships Between "Society", "Organism" and "Being"', in Georges

Bataille, *The College of Sociology*, trans. Betsey Wing (Minneapolis: University of Minnesota Press, 1988), pp. 73–84.
13 Michel Serres, *The Natural Contract*, trans. Elizabeth MacArthur and William Paulson (Ann Arbor: University of Michigan Press, 1995), p. 25.
14 F. David Peat, 'Interview with David Bohm', available at www.fdavidpeat.com/interviews/bohm.htm (accessed 17 December 2010).
15 Rilke, *The Poetry of Rilke*, pp. 526–7.

1 Meetings – Conversations on War and Peace

1 See Bertolt Brecht, *Werke; grosse kommentierte Berliner und Frankfurter Ausgabe Bertolt Brecht 1898–1956*, ed. Werner Hecht (Frankfurt and Berlin: Suhrkamp and Aufbau-Verlag, 2003), vols 28–30; Bertolt Brecht, 'Open Letter to German Artists and Writers', in Tom Kuhn, Steve Giles and Laura J.R. Bradley (eds), *Bertolt Brecht 1898–1956* (London: Methuen, 2003), p. 318.
2 Charles Chaplin, *My Autobiography* (London: Penguin, 2003), pp. 393–5.

2 Inventing Peace

1 See George Orwell, *1984* (Oxford: Oxford University Press, 1984). Orwell's *1984* was first published in 1949.
2 Bertolt Brecht, *Mother Courage and her Children*, trans. John Willett (London: Methuen Drama, 1983), pp. 3–4.
3 See William James, 'The Moral Equivalent of War', in William James, *Memories and Studies* (New York: Greenwood Press, 1968), pp. 265–96.
4 William James, 'Remarks at the Peace Banquet', in James, *Memories and Studies*, pp. 305–6.
5 Ibid., p. 303; original emphasis.
6 Ibid., p. 301.
7 See Henri Bergson, *Matter and Memory*, trans. Nancy Margaret Paul and W. Scott Palmer (New York: Zone Books, 1991).
8 Henri Bergson, *The Creative Mind: An Introduction to Metaphysics*, trans. Mabelle L. Andison (New York: Citadel Press, 1992), p. 51.
9 Bergson's notion of matter and memory has been controversial; in particular his notion of time has been seen to be at odds with cinema. Bergson was critical of the emerging art of cinema: he thought cinema, like 'knowledge', presented a partial truth. However, as the philosopher Gilles Deleuze points out, Bergson is often contradictory across texts – for example, this difference is expressed in Bergson's *Matter and Memory* and *The Creative Mind*; in effect his writing on time offers a way of considering cinematic time and movement. See Gilles Deleuze, *Cinema 1: The Movement-Image*, trans. Barbara Habberjam and Hugh Tomlinson (Minneapolis: University of Minnesota Press, 1986) and *Cinema 2: The Time-*

Image, trans. Hugh Tomlinson and Robert Galeta (London: Continuum, 1989).
10 In the Fifties, Bachelard wrote a book, *The Dialectic of Duration*, as a critical response to Bergson's idea of duration and time. Although Bachelard agreed with Bergson's fundamental premise of lived time, he argued that time is interrupted by the events of this world. For Bachelard, what is at stake is how we understand a philosophy of repose and a philosophy of continuity and movement. As Bachelard notes, the idea of duration is 'intended to be an introduction to the teaching of a philosophy of repose'. Bachelard is one of the few philosophers to seriously consider stillness, tranquillity and repose in our habits of mind and culture. See Gaston Bachelard, *The Dialectic of Duration*, trans. Mary McAllester Jones (Manchester: Clinamen Press, 2000), p. 17.
11 See Gaston Bachelard, *The Poetics of Reverie*, trans. Daniel Russell (Boston: Beacon Press, 1971).
12 Ibid., p. 176.
13 See Henri Bergson, *The Two Sources of Morality and Religion* (Notre Dame, IN: University of Notre Dame Press, 2006).
14 In their different ways, James Joyce and Marcel Proust offer accounts of memory that reconsider language as well as time and presence. See James Joyce, *Ulysses* (London: Penguin Classics, 2000) and *A Portrait of the Artist as a Young Man* (New York: Premier Classics, 2006). See Marcel Proust, *Remembrance of Things Past: Volume 1*, trans. C.K. Scott Moncrieff and Terence Kilmartin (London: Penguin Books, 1989).
15 Martin Buber, *I and Thou*, trans. Ronald Gregor Smith (London and New York: Continuum, 2004), p. 18.
16 'Ash Wednesday' was first published in 1930.
17 T.S. Eliot, 'Ash Wednesday', in T.S. Eliot, *Collected Poems, 1909–1962* (London: Faber and Faber, 2002), pp. 94–5.
18 Martin Buber, *The Way of Response*, ed. N.N. Glatzer (New York: Schocken Books, 1966), p. 22.
19 Robert Bresson, *Notes on the Cinematographer*, trans. Jonathan Griffin (Copenhagen: Green Integer Books, 1997), p. 16.
20 See Albert Camus, *The Rebel*, trans. Anthony Bower (London: Penguin Books, 2000).
21 John Berger, *Sense of Sight* (London: Vintage, 1993), p. 295.
22 Rather than the famous dictum of Jean Paul Sartre that 'essence precedes existence,' Serres states that 'relationships come before being.' See Mary Zournazi and Michel Serres, 'The Art of Living', in Mary Zournazi, *Hope – New Philosophies for Change* (Routledge: New York, 2003), pp. 192–209.
23 Martin Buber, *Between Man and Man*, trans. Ronald Gregor Smith (London and New York: Routledge Classics, 2002), p. 12.

24 See David Bohm, *Wholeness and the Implicate Order* (London and New York: Routledge, 1980).
25 We use the *I–You* translation of *Ich–Du* as it relates closer to the informality of the original German usage. However, we use Smith's 1937 overall translation as it reads more precisely to the issues that we address and with Buber's original text from 1923. Where necessary for sense and context we keep the original *I–Thou*.
26 Buber, *I and Thou*, p. 11.
27 See Immanuel Kant, 'Eternal Peace', in Howard P. Kainz (ed.), *Philosophical Perspectives on Peace* (Athens, OH: Ohio University Press, 1987), pp. 65–86.
28 Buber, *I and Thou*, pp. 19–20.
29 Ibid., pp. 20–1.
30 Andrei Tarkovsky, *Sculpting in Time*, trans. Kitty Hunter-Blair (Austin: University of Texas Press, 1986), p. 68.
31 Ibid., pp. 25–6.
32 Ibid., p. 110.
33 Martin Buber, 'Genuine Dialogue and the Possibilities of Peace', in Martin Buber, *Pointing the Way: Collected Essays*, ed. and trans. Maurice Friedman (London: Routledge and Kegan Paul, 1957), p. 235.

3 Enduring Images

1 See Paul Schrader, *Transcendental Style in Film: Ozu, Bresson, Dreyer* (Berkeley: University of California Press, 1972); Donald Richie, *Ozu* (Los Angeles and London: University of California Press, 1974).
2 Schrader, *Transcendental Style in Film*, p. 3.
3 Ozu, cited in Richie, *Ozu*, p. 188.
4 Ozu, cited in Donald Richie, 'Introduction', in Yasujiro Ozu and Kogo Noda, *Tokyo Story: The Ozu/Noda Screenplay*, trans. Donald Richie and Eric Klestadt (Berkeley: Stone Bridge Press, 2003), p. 18.
5 See the Select Filmography for each film's release date.
6 Gaston Bachelard, *The Poetics of Reverie*, trans. Daniel Russell (Boston: Beacon Press, 1971), p. 118.
7 Sogyal Rinpoche, *The Tibetan Book of Living and Dying* (London and Sydney: Rider, 1998), p. 25.
8 See David Bordwell's discussion of Ozu, and his argument around Ozu's historical poetics in *Ozu and the Poetics of Cinema* (Princeton: Princeton University Press, 1988).
9 See James Hillman, *A Blue Fire: Selected Writings by James Hillman* (New York: Harper Perennial, 1991).
10 Ozu and Noda, *Tokyo Story*, pp. 94–6.
11 Ozu and Noda, *Tokyo Story*, p. 71.
12 Schrader, *Transcendental Style in Film*, p. 164.

13 Mircea Eliade, *The Sacred and the Profane*, trans. William R. Trask (Orlando: Harcourt, 1987), p. 30, original emphasis.
14 Schrader, *Transcendental Style in Film*, p. 28.
15 Martin Buber, *I and Thou*, trans. Ronald Gregor Smith (London and New York: Continuum, 2004), p. 17.
16 Ozu and Noda, *Tokyo Story*, pp. 126–7.
17 Yasujiro Ozu, *Carnets, 1933–1963*, trans. Josiane Pinon-Kawataké (France: Editions Alive, 1993), pp. 630–1, 639, 647. These entries come from the French translation of Ozu's diaries; all translations into the English are by Wim Wenders.

4 Imagining the Real

1 See Jane Bennett's account of 'enchantment' in *The Enchantment of Modern Life* (Princeton: Princeton University Press, 2001).
2 See James Hillman's *Terrible Love of War* (New York: Penguin, 2004).
3 W.H. Auden, *Poems* (London: Faber and Faber, 2005), p. 28.
4 John Berger, *and our faces, my heart, brief as photos* (London: Bloomsbury, 2005), p. 21.
5 Ibid., p. 89.
6 Rainer Maria Rilke, *The Poetry of Rilke*, ed. and trans. Edward Snow (New York: North Point Press, 2009), p. 359.
7 Gaston Bachelard suggests that instead of the Oedipus complex we should speak of the 'Orpheus complex'. He writes: 'This complex would correspond to our first and fundamental need to give pleasure and to offer solace; it would be revealed in the caresses of tender sympathy, and characterised by the attitude in which our being gains pleasure through giving pleasure, by the attitude of making some offering . . .' See Gaston Bachelard, *The Dialectic of Duration*, trans. Mary McAllester Jones (Manchester: Clinamen Press, 2000), p. 152. Suffice to say, we cannot develop the idea of the 'Orpheus complex' here, but it is worth noting for future work on a philosophy of repose and identity.
8 Margaret Somerville has written on the 'ethical imagination' as well as the consideration of how to imagine a shared ethics and community. See Margaret Somerville, *The Ethical Imagination* (Melbourne: Melbourne University Press, 2007). See also Iris Murdoch for work on imagination, ethics and the 'good'. Iris Murdoch, *The Sovereignty of Good* (London and New York: Routledge Classics, 2007).
9 Emmanuel Levinas, cited in Jacques Derrida, 'Adieu', *Critical Inquiry* 23/1 (Autumn 1996), p. 4.
10 See Emmanuel Levinas, *Time and the Other*, trans. Richard A. Cohen (Pittsburgh: Duquesne University Press, 1987).

11 See Mary Zournazi and Michel Serres, 'The Art of Living', in Mary Zournazi, *Hope – New Philosophies for Change* (New York: Routledge, 2003), pp. 192–209.
12 See Micrea Eliade, *The Sacred and the Profane*, trans. William R. Trask (Orlando: Harcourt, 1987).
13 Guy Debord's work on the society of the spectacle provides for an interesting look at the sacred and illusion, how the whole of the social world is built on spectacle and desire. See Guy Debord, *Society of the Spectacle* (Detroit: Black & Red, 1983).
14 Eliade, *The Sacred and the Profane*, pp. 12–13, original emphasis.
15 Simone Weil, 'The *Iliad*, or the Poem of Force', trans. Mary McCarthy, in Simone Weil, *War and the Iliad* (New York: New York Review Books, 2005), p. 3.
16 Weil, 'The *Iliad*, or the Poem of Force', p. 14, original emphasis.
17 Ibid., pp. 25–6.
18 Ibid., p. 37.
19 René Girard, *Violence and the Sacred*, trans. Patrick Gregory (London and New York: Continuum, 2008).
20 Cited in René Girard, 'The Nonsacrificial Death of Christ' in René Girard, *The Girard Reader*, ed. James G. Williams (New York: Crossroad Publishing Company, 1996), p. 187.
21 Weil, 'The *Iliad*, or the Poem of Force', p. 11.
22 Roland Barthes made a similar point in his *Le Monde* review of *Salò* in 1976. For an English version, see Roland Barthes, 'Pasolini's *Salò*: Sade to the Letter', in Paul Willemen (ed.), *Pier Paolo Pasolini* (London: British Film Institute, 1977), pp. 64–6.
23 Marker's *AK* is a documentary film on the making of Kurosawa's *Ran*.
24 Akira Kurosawa, *Something Like an Autobiography*, trans. Audie E. Bock (New York: Alfred A. Knopf, 1983), p. 54.
25 See Rowan Williams' book, *Christ on Trial* (London: HarperCollins Religious, 2000), for his discussion of 'hospitality for the truth' as an invitation toward understanding and compassion. Williams argues that this hospitality is a necessary condition in times of violence.
26 Girard, 'The Nonsacrificial Death of Christ', pp. 187–8.
27 T.S. Eliot, *Four Quartets* (London: Faber and Faber, 2001), pp. 41–2. *Four Quartets* was first published in 1943.
28 Ibid., p. 17.
29 *Day of Wrath* was released in 1943. In some ways, the film is a reflection more broadly on the persecution and injustice that occurred toward Jews, women and minority groups during World War Two.
30 Carl Dreyer, *Dreyer in Double Reflection: Dreyer's Writing About Film*, ed. Donald Skoller (New York: Dutton, 1973), p. 129.

31 Paul Schrader's discussion of Ozu, Bresson and Dreyer gives very good insights into the cinematic architecture of each of these directors and their unique styles. Paul Schrader, *Transcendental Style in Film: Ozu, Bresson, Dreyer* (Berkeley: University of California Press, 1972).
32 Dreyer has spoken of his use of backgrounds and 'light' to animate scenes. We see his use of light in its most surreal and experimental forms in his 1932 film *Vampyr*. See Dreyer, *Dreyer in Double Reflection*. François Truffaut also comments on Dreyer's 'whiteness': '... in *Ordet*, white predominates again, this time a milky whiteness, the whiteness of sun-drenched curtains, something we have never seen before or since.' See François Truffaut, 'The Whiteness of Carl Dreyer', in François Truffaut, *The Films in my Life* (New York: Da Capo Press, 1994), p. 49.
33 Simone Weil, *Gravity and Grace*, trans. Emma Crawford and Mario von der Ruhr (London and New York: Routledge Classics, 2006), p. 11.
34 Cited in Richard A. Cohen's translator's introduction in Levinas, *Time and the Other*, p. 24.
35 Émile Durkheim, *The Elementary Forms of Religious Life*, trans. Carol Cosman (Oxford: Oxford University Press, 2001), pp. 28–9.
36 Gaston Bachelard, *The Poetics of Reverie*, trans. Daniel Russell (Boston: Beacon Press, 1971), p. 185, original emphasis.

5 Which Future of Seeing?

1 See Paul Virilio, *War and Cinema: The Logistics of Perception*, trans. Patrick Camiller (London and New York: Verso, 1984), and *Speed and Politics: An Essay in Dromology*, trans. Mark Polizzotti (New York: Semiotext(e), 1986).
2 Cited in Wim Wenders, *My Time with Antonioni*, trans. Michael Hoffman (London and New York: Faber and Faber, 2000), p. x.
3 See Martin Heidegger, 'A Question Concerning Technology', in Martin Heidegger, *Basic Writings Martin Heidegger*, trans. William Lovitt (London and New York: Routledge, 1993), pp. 311–41.
4 See David Bohm, *On Dialogue* (London and New York: Routledge Classics, 2004).
5 See also David Bohm, *Wholeness and the Implicate Order* (London and New York: Routledge, 1980).
6 It is hard to give a brief descriptor to Roland Barthes; he was an enigmatic figure as well as a brilliant writer, philosopher, and semiotician.
7 Roland Barthes, *Camera Lucida: Reflections on Photography*, trans. Richard Howard (London: Vintage, 1993). *Camera Lucida* was first published in 1979.
8 Ibid., p. 81.
9 Ibid., p. 70.
10 Ibid., p. 87.

notes   203

11 Susan Sontag, *Regarding the Pain of Others* (London and New York: Penguin, 2003).
12 Italian filmmaker Federico Fellini spoke of cinema at its best as a type of sincerity; cinema can be a *sincere witness* of human experience. See Fellini's 'autobiographical' film, *Fellini un autoritratto ritrovato* (*Fellini Narrates: A Discovered Self-Portrait*), 2000.
13 Gaston Bachelard, *The Poetics of Reverie*, trans. Daniel Russell (Boston: Beacon Press, 1971), p. 120, original emphasis.
14 Martin Buber, *I and Thou*, trans. Ronald Gregor Smith (London and New York: Continuum, 2004), p. 15.
15 John Berger, *The Shape of a Pocket* (London: Bloomsbury, 2001), p. 22.
16 Robert Bresson, *Notes on the Cinematographer*, trans. Jonathan Griffin (Copenhagen: Green Integer Books, 1997), p. 130.
17 Bresson, *Notes on the Cinematographer*, p. 14.
18 Ibid., p. 93.
19 Cited in Paul Schrader, *Transcendental Style in Film: Ozu, Bresson, Dreyer* (Berkeley: University of California Press, 1972), p. 61.
20 Bresson, *Notes on the Cinematographer*, pp. 80–1.
21 Michelangelo Antonioni, *The Architecture of Vision*, ed. Marga Cottino-Jones (New York: Marisilio Publishers, 1996), p. 95.
22 *The Passenger* was first released in 1975.
23 Antonioni, *The Architecture of Vision*, p. 51.
24 Ibid.
25 Cited in Emmanuel Levinas, *Ethics and Infinity*, trans. Richard A. Cohen (Pittsburgh: Duquesne University Press, 1994), p. 101.
26 Emmanuel Levinas, *Difficult Freedom*, trans. Sean Hand (Baltimore: Johns Hopkins University Press, 1997), p. 155.
27 Buber, *I and Thou*, p. 14.
28 Who could forget Tarkovsky's image of a tree at the end of his 1986 film *Offret* (*The Sacrifice*)?
29 Rainer Maria Rilke, *The Poetry of Rilke*, ed. and trans. Edward Snow (New York: North Point Press, 2009), pp. 76–7. 'Apprehension' was originally published in 1902 and was a response to the rapid industrialisation of the nineteenth and early twentieth centuries.
30 Simone Weil, *Gravity and Grace*, trans. Emma Crawford and Mario von der Ruhr (London and New York: Routledge Classics, 2006), p. 150.
31 Rilke, *The Poetry of Rilke*, pp. 222–3. 'Archaic Torso of Apollo' was first published in 1908.

Bibliography

Antonioni, Michelangelo, *The Architecture of Vision*, ed. Marga Cottino-Jones (New York: Marisilio Publishers, 1996).
Arendt, Hannah, *Eichmann in Jerusalem: A Report on the Banality of Evil* (New York: Penguin Books, 1963).
—— *On Violence* (New York: Harcourt Bruce and Company, 1969).
Auden, W.H., 'Forgotten Laughter, Forgotten Prayer', *New York Times*, 2 February 1971, p. 37.
—— *Poems* (London: Faber and Faber, 2000).
Bachelard, Gaston, *The Poetics of Reverie*, trans. Daniel Russell (Boston: Beacon Press, 1971).
—— *On Poetic Imagination and Reverie*, trans. Colette Gaudin (Dallas: Spring Publications, 1987).
—— *The Poetics of Space*, trans. Maria Jolas (Boston: Beacon Press, 1994).
—— *The Dialectic of Duration*, trans. Mary McAllester Jones (Manchester: Clinamen Press, 2000).
—— *Earth and Reveries of Will: An Essay on the Imagination of Matter*, trans. Kenneth Haltman (Dallas: Dallas Institute Publications, 2002).
Bachmann, Gideon, 'A Love Today: An Interview with Michelangelo Antonioni', *Film Quarterly* 36/4 (Summer 1983), pp. 1–14.
Baker, Nicholson, *Human Smoke: The Beginnings of World War II, The End of Civilization* (London: Pocket Books, 2009).
Bakhtin, Mikhail, *The Dialogic Imagination*, trans. Caryl Emerson and Michael Holquist (Austin: University of Texas Press, 1981).
Balázs, Béla, 'Visible Man, or the Culture of Film', *Screen* 48/1 (2007), pp. 91–108.
Barthes, Roland, 'Pasolini's *Salo*: Sade to the Letter', in Paul Willemen (ed.), *Pier Paolo Pasolini* (London: British Film Institute, 1977), pp. 64–6.
—— *Camera Lucida: Reflections on Photography*, trans. Richard Howard (London: Vintage, 1993).
—— *The Neutral*, trans. Rosalind E. Krauss and Denis Hollier (New York: Columbia University Press, 2005).
Bataille, Georges and Roger Caillois, 'Sacred Sociology and the Relationships between "Society", "Organism" and "Being"', in Georges Bataille, *The*

bibliography

College of Sociology, trans. Betsey Wing (Minneapolis: University of Minnesota Press, 1988), pp. 73–84.

Bateson, Gregory, *Steps to an Ecology of Mind* (Chicago and London: University of Chicago Press, 2000).

—— and Mary Catherine Bateson, *Angels Fear: Towards an Epistemology of the Sacred* (Creskill, NJ: Hampton Press, 2005).

Bazin, André, *What Is Cinema? Volume Two*, trans. Hugh Gray (Berkeley: University of California Press, 2004).

—— *What Is Cinema? Volume One*, trans. Hugh Gray (Berkeley: University of California Press, 2005).

Benjamin, Walter, *Illuminations*, trans. Harry Zohn (London: Fontana Press, 1991).

Bennett, Jane, *The Enchantment of Modern Life* (Princeton, NJ: Princeton University Press, 2001).

Berger, John, *Sense of Sight* (London: Vintage, 1993).

—— *The Shape of a Pocket* (London: Bloomsbury, 2001).

—— *and our faces, my heart, brief as photos* (London: Bloomsbury, 2005).

—— *Ways of Seeing* (London: BBC and Penguin Books, 2008).

Bergson, Henri, *The Meaning of War*, intro. H. Wildon Carr (London: T. Fisher Unwin, 1915).

—— *Matter and Memory*, trans. Nancy Margaret Paul and W. Scott Palmer (New York: Zone Books, 1991).

—— *The Creative Mind: An Introduction to Metaphysics*, trans. Mabelle L. Andison (New York: Citadel Press, 1992).

—— *Creative Evolution*, trans. Arthur Mitchell (New York: Dover Publications, 1998).

—— *Time and Free Will*, trans. F.L. Pogson (New York: Dover Publications, 2001).

—— *The Two Sources of Morality and Religion* (Notre Dame, IN: University of Notre Dame Press, 2006).

Blanchot, Maurice, *The Writing of Disaster*, trans. Ann Smock (Lincoln, NB, and London: University of Nebraska Press, 1986).

Bohm, David, *Wholeness and the Implicate Order* (London and New York: Routledge, 1980).

—— *On Dialogue* (London and New York: Routledge Classics, 2004).

—— *On Creativity* (London and New York: Routledge Classics, 2005).

Bordwell, David, *Ozu and the Poetics of Cinema* (Princeton: Princeton University Press, 1988).

Brecht, Bertolt, *Mother Courage and her Children*, trans. John Willett (London: Methuen Drama, 1983).

—— *Werke; grosse kommentierte Berliner und Frankfurter Ausgabe Bertolt Brecht 1898–1956*, ed. Werner Hecht (Frankfurt and Berlin: Suhrkamp and Aufbau-Verlag, 2003), vols 28–30.

—— 'Open Letter to German Artists and Writers', in Tom Kuhn, Steve Giles and Laura J.R. Bradley (eds), *Bertolt Brecht 1898–1956* (London: Methuen 2003), p. 318.

Bresson, Robert, *Notes on the Cinematographer*, trans. Jonathan Griffin (Copenhagen: Green Integer Books, 1997).

Brunette, Peter, *The Films of Michelangelo Antonioni* (Cambridge: Cambridge University Press, 1998).

Buber, Martin, *Images of Good and Evil*, trans. Michael Bullock (London: Routledge and Kegan Paul, 1952).

—— *Pointing the Way: Collected Essays*, ed. and trans. Maurice Friedman (London: Routledge and Kegan Paul, 1957).

—— *The Way of Response*, ed. N.N. Glatzer (New York: Schocken Books, 1966).

—— *Eclipse of God*, trans. Gottefinsternis (New York: Green Press, 1977).

—— *Between Man and Man*, trans. Ronald Gregor Smith (London and New York: Routledge Classics, 2002).

—— *Meetings: Autobiographical Fragments*, ed. and trans. Maurice Friedman. (London and New York: Routledge, 2002).

—— *The Way of Man*, intro. Julia Neuberger (London and New York: Routledge Classics, 2002).

—— *I and Thou*, trans. Ronald Gregor Smith (London and New York: Continuum, 2004).

Camus, Albert, *The Rebel*, trans. Anthony Bower (London: Penguin Books, 2000).

Conrad, Joseph, *Heart of Darkness* (London: Penguin Modern Classics, 1973).

Curtis, Adela M., *The Way of Silence* (London: School of Meditation, 1932), vols 1–7.

Daney, Serge, *Postcards from the Cinema*, trans. Paul Douglas Grant (New York: Berg, 2007).

Debord, Guy, *Society of the Spectacle* (Detroit: Black & Red, 1983).

Deleuze, Gilles, *Cinema 1: The Movement-Image*, trans. Barbara Habberjam and Hugh Tomlinson (Minneapolis: University of Minnesota Press, 1986).

—— *Cinema 2: The Time-Image*, trans Hugh Tomlinson and Robert Galeta (London: Continuum, 1989).

—— *Bergsonism*, trans. Hugh Tomlinson and Barbara Habberjam (New York: Zone Books, 1991).

Derrida, Jacques, 'Adieu', *Critical Inquiry* 23/1 (Autumn 1996), pp. 1–10.

Dewey, John, *Art as Experience* (New York: Perigee Books, 2005).

Dillard, Annie, *Pilgrim at Tinker Creek* (New York: Harper's Magazine Press, 1974).

Dostoyevsky, Fyodor, *Crime and Punishment*, trans. David McDuff (London: Penguin Books, 1991).

Dreyer, Carl Theodor, *Dreyer in Double Reflection: Dreyer's Writing About Film*, ed. Donald Skoller (New York: Dutton, 1973).

Durkheim, Émile, *The Elementary Forms of Religious Life*, trans. Carol Cosman (Oxford: Oxford University Press, 2001).
Einstein, Albert and Sigmund Freud, 'Why War?', in Sigmund Freud, *Civilization, Society and Religion*, Freud Penguin Library Volume 12 (London: Penguin, 1991), pp. 341–62.
Eliade, Mircea, *The Myth of the Eternal Return or, Cosmos and History*, trans. Willard R. Trask (Princeton: Princeton University Press, 1971).
—— *The Sacred and the Profane*, trans. William R. Trask (Orlando: Harcourt, 1987).
Eliot, T.S., *Four Quartets* (London: Faber and Faber, 2001).
—— 'Ash Wednesday', in T.S. Eliot, *Collected Poems, 1909–1962* (London: Faber and Faber, 2002), pp. 94–5.
—— *Collected Poems, 1909–1962* (London: Faber and Faber, 2002).
Ellul, Jacques, *The Technological Society*, trans. John Wilkinson (New York: Vintage Books, 1964).
Epstein, Mark, *Thoughts Without a Thinker* (New York: Basic Books, 1995).
Foucault, Michel, *Care of the Self: History of Sexuality, Volume 3*, trans. Robert Hurley (London: Penguin Books, 1990).
Forster, E.M., *Aspects of the Novel* (London: Edward Arnold, 1927).
Gilliat, Penelope, *Jean Renoir: Essays, Conversations, Reviews* (New York: McGraw Hill Books, 1975).
Girard, René, *The Girard Reader*, ed. James G. Williams (New York: Crossroad Publishing Company, 1996).
—— 'The Nonsacrificial Death of Christ', in René Girard, *The Girard Reader*, ed. James G. Williams (New York: Crossroad Publishing Company, 1996), pp. 177–88.
—— *Violence and the Sacred*, trans. Patrick Gregory (London and New York: Continuum, 2008).
Godard, Jean-Luc and Maurice Merleau-Ponty, 'The Testimony of Balthazar', *Cahiers du Cinema in English*, 6 (December 1966), pp. 44–5.
—— and Michel Delahaye, 'The Question: Interview with Robert Bresson', trans. Jane Pease, in. James Quandt (ed.), *Robert Bresson* (Ontario: Toronto International Film Festival Group, 1998), pp. 452–83.
Goethe, Johann Wolfgang, *Theory of Colours* (Boston and London: MIT Press, 1970).
Hart, Dakin, 'Peace and Love Picasso', in John Richardson (ed.), *Picasso Mosqueteros* (New York: Gagosian Gallery, 2009), pp. 239–71.
Heidegger, Martin, 'Building Dwelling Thinking', in Martin Heidegger, *Poetry, Language, Thought*, ed. and trans. Albert Hofstadter (New York: Harper and Row, 1975), pp. 143–61.
—— 'A Question Concerning Technology', in Martin Heidegger, *Basic Writings Martin Heidegger*, trans. William Lovitt (London and New York: Routledge, 1993), pp. 311–41.

Herrigal, Eugene, *Zen in the Art of Archery* (London: Arkana Book, 1985).
Hillman, James, *A Blue Fire: Selected Writings by James Hillman* (New York: Harper Perennial, 1991).
—— *A Terrible Love of War* (New York: Penguin, 2004).
Homer, *The Iliad*, trans. Robert Fables (London: Penguin Classics, 2001).
Huxley, Aldous, *The Perennial Philosophy* (London: Chatto & Windus, 1957).
Iqbal, Muhammad, *Shikwa and Jawab-i-Shikwa Compliant and Answer: Iqbal's Dialogue with Allah*, trans. Khushwant Singh (Oxford: Oxford University Press, 1981).
James, William, *The Meaning of Truth* (London and New York: Longmans, Green and Co., 1909).
—— 'The Moral Equivalent of War', in William James, *Memories and Studies* (New York: Greenwood Press, 1968), pp. 265–96.
—— 'Remarks at the Peace Banquet', in William James, *Memories and Studies* (New York: Greenwood Press, 1968), pp. 297–306.
—— *Essays in Radical Empiricism* (New York: Dover Publications, 2003).
—— *The Varieties of Religious Experience: A Study in Human Nature* (New York and London: Routledge Classics, 2008).
Joyce, James, *Ulysses* (London: Penguin Classics, 2000).
—— *A Portrait of the Artist as a Young Man* (New York: Premier Classics, 2006).
Jung, Carl, *Four Archetypes* (London and New York: Routledge Classics, 2003).
Kandinsky, Wassily, *Concerning the Spiritual in Art* (New York: George Wittenborn Inc., 1976).
Kant, Immanuel, 'Eternal Peace', in Howard P. Kainz (ed.), *Philosophical Perspectives on Peace* (Athens, OH: Ohio University Press, 1987), pp. 65–86.
Klee, Paul, *Notebooks, Volume 1: The Thinking Eye*, ed. Jürg Spiller, trans. Ralph Manheim (London: Lund Humphries, 1961).
Kristeva, Julia, *Proust and the Sense of Time*, trans. Stephen Bann (London: Faber and Faber, 1993).
Kurosawa, Akira, *Something Like an Autobiography*, trans. Audie E. Bock (New York: Alfred A. Knopf, 1983).
Lakoff, George, *Don't Think of An Elephant: Know Your Values and Frame the Debate* (Melbourne: Scribe, 2005).
Latour, Bruno, *War of the Worlds: What About Peace?* (Chicago: Prickly Paradigm Press, 2002).
—— 'Whose Cosmos, Which Cosmopolitics? Comments on the Peace Terms of Ulrick Beck', *Common Knowledge* 10/3 (2004), pp. 450–62.
Leeuw, Gerardus van der, *Sacred and Profane Beauty: The Holy in Art*, trans. David E. Green (London: Weidenfeld and Nicolson, 1963).
Levinas, Emmanuel, *Time and the Other*, trans. Richard A. Cohen (Pittsburgh: Duquesne University Press, 1987).

—— 'Reality and its Shadow', trans. Alphonso Lingis, in Sean Hand (ed.), *The Levinas Reader* (Oxford: Basil Blackwell, 1989), pp. 129–43.
—— *Ethics and Infinity*, trans. Richard A. Cohen (Pittsburgh: Duquesne University Press, 1994).
—— *In the Time of the Nations*, trans. Michael B. Smith (Bloomington and Indianapolis: Indiana University Press, 1994).
—— *Totality and Infinity*, trans. Alphonso Lingis (Duquesne University Press: Pittsburgh, 1995).
—— *Difficult Freedom*, trans. Sean Hand (Baltimore: Johns Hopkins University Press, 1997).
—— 'Peace and Proximity', in Robert Bernasconi, Simon Critchley and Adriaan T. Peperzak (eds), *Emmanuel Levinas: Basic Philosophical Writings* (Bloomington and Indianapolis: Indiana University Press, 2008), pp. 161–70.
Manvich, Lee, *Digital Cinema and the History of a Moving Image* (Cambridge, MA: MIT Press, 2001).
Maritain, Jacques, *The Social and Political Philosophy of Jacques Maritain: Selected Readings*, ed. Joseph W. Evans and Leo R. Ward (London: Geoffrey Bles, 1956).
—— *The Responsibility of the Artist* (Charles Scribner's Sons: New York, 1960).
Merleau-Ponty, Maurice, *The Primacy of Perception*, ed. James M. Edie (Evanston, IL: Northwestern University Press, 1964).
—— *Sense and Non-Sense*, ed. and trans. Hubert L. Dreyfus and Patricia Allen Dreyfus (Evanston, IL: Northwestern University Press, 1964).
—— *Phenomenology, Language and Sociology: Selected essays of Maurice Merleau-Ponty*, ed. John O'Neill (London: Heinemann, 1974).
—— *The Visible and Invisible*, trans. Alphonso Lingis (Evanston, IL: Northwestern University Press, 1987).
—— *Phenomenology of Perception*, trans. Colin Smith (London and New York: Routledge Classics, 2005).
Merton, Thomas, *Peace in a Post-Christian Era*, ed. Patricia A. Burton (New York: Orbis Books, 2004).
McLuhan, Malcolm, *Understanding Media: The Extensions of Man* (New York: McGraw Hill, 1964).
Mosès, Stéphane, *System and Revelation: The Philosophy of Franz Rosenzweig*, trans. Catherine Tihanyi (Detroit: Wayne State University Press, 1992).
Murdoch, Iris, *The Sovereignty of Good* (London and New York: Routledge Classics, 2007).
Nouwen, Henri, *The Wounded Healer* (New York: Image Books, 1979).
Oppler, Ellen, *Picasso's Guernica* (New York: Norton, 1988).
Orwell, George, 'You and the Atomic Bomb', *Tribune*, 19 October 1945, pp. 7–8.
—— *1984* (Oxford: Oxford University Press, 1984).

Otto, Rudolf, *The Idea of the Holy*, trans. John W. Harvey (Oxford: Oxford University Press, 1958).
Ozu, Yasujiro, *Carnets, 1933–1963*, trans. Josiane Pinon-Kawataké (France: Editions Alive, 1993)
—— and Noda Kogo, *Tokyo Story: The Ozu/Noda Screenplay*, trans. Donald Richie and Eric Klestadt (Berkeley: Stone Bridge Press, 2003).
Peat, David F., 'Interview with David Bohm', available at www.fdavidpeat.com/interviews/bohm.htm (accessed 17 December 2010).
Phillips, Adam and Barbara Taylor, *On Kindness* (London: Penguin Books, 2009).
Prince, Stephen, *The Warrior's Camera: The Cinema of Akira Kurosawa* (Princeton: Princeton University Press, 1999).
Proust, Marcel, *Remembrance of Things Past, Volume 1*, trans. C.K. Scott Moncrieff and Terence Kilmartin (London: Penguin Books, 1989).
Quandt, James (ed.), *Robert Bresson* (Ontario: Toronto International Film Festival Group, 1988).
The Qur'an, trans. J.M. Rodwell (London: Phoenix, 1994).
Rancière, Jacques, *The Future of Images*, trans. Gregory Elliott (London and New York: Verso, 2007).
Renoir, Jean, *Renoir on Renoir*, trans. Carol Volk (Cambridge: Cambridge University Press, 1989).
Richie, Donald, *Ozu* (Los Angeles and London: University of California Press, 1974).
—— *The Films of Akira Kurosawa* (Los Angeles and London: University of California Press, 1996).
—— 'Introduction', in Yasujiro Ozu and Kogo Noda, *Tokyo Story: The Ozu/Noda Screenplay*, trans. Donald Richie and Eric Klestadt (Berkeley: Stone Bridge Press, 2003).
Rilke, Rainer Maria, *Duino Elegies*, trans. David Young (New York and London: W.W. Norton & Co., 2006).
—— *The Poetry of Rilke*, ed. and trans. Edward Snow (New York: North Point Press, 2009).
Rinpoche, Sogyal, *The Tibetan Book of Living and Dying* (London and Sydney: Rider, 1998).
Rodriguez, Richard, '"The God of the Desert": Jerusalem and the Ecology of Monotheism', *Harper's Magazine*, January 2008, pp. 35–46.
Rosenzweig, Franz, *The Star of Redemption*, trans. William W. Hallo (Notre Dame, IN: University of Notre Dame Press, 1985).
Salgado, Sebastião, *Africa* (London and Los Angeles: Taschen, 2007).
Sardar, Ziauddin, *Reading the Qur'an: The Contemporary Relevance of the Sacred Text of Islam* (London: Hurst & Company, 2011).
Sartre, Jean-Paul, *Being and Nothingness*, trans. Hazel E. Barnes (New York and London: Pocket Books, 1966).

bibliography

—— *The Imaginary: Phenomenological Psychology of the Imagination*, trans. Jonathan Webber (London and New York: Routledge Classics, 2004).
Schepher-Hughes, Nancy and Philippe Bourgois (eds), *Violence in War and Peace: An Anthology* (London: Blackwell, 2004).
Schrader, Paul, *Transcendental Style in Film: Ozu, Bresson, Dreyer* (Berkeley: University of California Press, 1972).
Sen'ichi, Hisamatsu, *The Vocabulary of Japanese Literary Aesthetics* (Toyko: Centre for East Asian Cultural Studies, 1963).
Sennett, Richard, *Authority* (London: Faber and Faber, 1980).
Serres, Michel, *Angels: A Modern Myth*, ed. Philippa Hurd, trans. Francis Cowper (Paris and New York: Flammarion, 1995).
—— *The Natural Contract*, trans. Elizabeth MacArthur and William Paulson (Ann Arbor: University of Michigan Press, 1995).
—— *Biogea*, trans. Randolph Burks (Minneapolis: Univocal Publishing, 2012).
Somerville, Margaret, *The Ethical Imagination* (Melbourne: Melbourne University Press, 2007).
Sontag, Susan, *Against Interpretation* (London: Vintage, 1994).
—— 'Spiritual Style in the Films of Robert Bresson', in James Quandt (ed.), *Robert Bresson* (Toronto: Toronto International Film Festival Group, 1998), pp. 57–71.
—— *Regarding the Pain of Others* (London and New York: Penguin, 2003).
Steindl-Rast, David and Sharon Lebell, *Music of Silence* (Berkeley: Seastone, 1998).
—— *Common Sense Spirituality* (New York: Crossroad Books, 2008).
Steiner, George, *Real Presences: Is There Anything in What We Say* (London: Faber and Faber, 1989).
Stevens, Wallace, *The Necessary Angel: Essays on Reality and the Imagination* (London: Faber and Faber, 1960).
Suzuki, David and Wayne Grady, *Tree: A Biography* (Sydney: Allen and Unwin, 2005).
Tarkovsky, Andrei, *Sculpting in Time*, trans. Kitty Hunter-Blair (Austin: University of Texas Press, 1986).
Thich Nhat Hanh, *Being Peace* (London and Sydney: Rider, 1987).
—— *Living Buddha, Living Christ* (New York: Riverhead Books, 2007).
Tolstoy, Leo, *War and Peace*, trans. Constance Garnett (New York: Modern Library, 2004).
Truffaut, François, *The Films in my Life* (New York: Da Capo Press, 1994).
—— 'The Whiteness of Carl Dreyer', in François Truffaut, *The Films in my Life* (New York: Da Capo Press, 1994), pp. 48–9.
Ud-Din Attar, Farid, *The Conference of the Birds*, trans. C.S. Nott (London: Routledge and Kegan Paul, 1964).
Valéry, Paul, *The Collected Works of Paul Valéry: Dialogues*, trans. W.M. Stewart (Princeton: Princeton University Press, 1971).

Vanier, Jean, *Finding Peace* (Toronto: Anansi Press, 2003).
—— *Becoming Human* (New York: Paulist Press, 2008).
Virilio, Paul, *War and Cinema: The Logistics of Perception*, trans. Patrick Camiller (London and New York: Verso, 1984).
—— *Speed and Politics: An Essay in Dromology*, trans. Mark Polizzotti (New York: Semiotext(e), 1986).
—— *Ground Zero*, trans. Chris Turner (London and New York: Verso, 2002).
Watts, Alan, *The Spirit of Zen* (London: John Murray, 1936).
Weil, Simone, *Simone Weil: An Anthology*, ed. Siân Miles (London: Virago Press, 1986).
—— 'The *Iliad*, or the Poem of Force', trans. Mary McCarthy, in Simone Weil, *War and The Iliad* (New York: New York Review Books, 2005), pp. 3–37.
—— *Gravity and Grace*, trans. Emma Crawford and Mario von der Ruhr (London and New York: Routledge Classics, 2006).
Wenders, Wim, *My Time with Antonioni*, trans. Michael Hoffman (London and New York: Faber and Faber, 2000).
—— *On Film: Essays and Conversations* (London: Faber and Faber, 2001).
—— *Once* (Munich: Schirmer/Mosel, 2001).
Whitehead North, Alfred, *Adventure of Ideas* (New York: The Free Press, 1967).
Williams, Rowan, *Christ on Trial* (London: HarperCollins Religious, 2000).
—— *Writing in the Dust: After September 11* (Michigan: William B. Eerdmans Publishing Company, 2002).
—— *Grace and Necessity: Reflections on Art and Love* (London: Continuum, 2005).
Winnicott, D.W., *Playing and Reality* (New York and London: Routledge, 2002).
Wolfflin, Heinrich, *Principles of Art History*, trans. M.D. Hottinger (New York: Dover Publications, 1950).
Zournazi, Mary, *Hope – New Philosophies for Change* (New York: Routledge, 2003).
—— *Keywords to War* (Melbourne: Scribe, 2007).
—— and Michel Serres, 'The Art of Living', in Mary Zournazi, *Hope – New Philosophies for Change* (New York: Routledge, 2003), pp. 192–209.

Select Filmography

Antonioni, Michelangelo
1960   *L'avventura (The Adventure)*
1961   *La Notte (The Night)*
1962   *L'Eclisse (Eclipse)*
1964   *Deserto rosso (Red Desert)*
1966   *Blowup*
1970   *Zabriskie Point*
1975   *The Passenger*

Bergman, Ingmar
1961   *Sasom I en Spegel (Through a Glass Darkly)*
1962   *Nattrardsgästerna (Winter Light)*

Bresson, Robert
1951   *Journal d'un curé de campagne (Diary of a Country Priest)*
1956   *Un condamné à mort s'est échappé ou Le vent souffle où il veut (A Man Escaped)*
1959   *Pickpocket*
1962   *Procès de Jeanne d'Arc (The Trial of Joan of Arc)*
1966   *Au hasard Balthazar*
1967   *Mouchette*
1983   *L'argent (Money)*

Chaplin, Charles
1940   *The Great Dictator*

Dreyer, Carl Theodor
1928   *La passion de Jeanne d'Arc (The Passion of Joan of Arc)*
1932   *Vampyr*
1943   *Vredens Day (Day of Wrath)*
1955   *Ordet (The Word)*

Fellini, Federico
2000 *Fellini un autoritratto ritrovato (Fellini Narrates: A Discovered Self-Portrait)*

Kurosawa, Akira
1951 *Hakuchi (The Idiot)*
1954 *Shichinin no Samurai (Seven Samurai)*
1985 *Ran (Chaos)*
1990 *Akira Kurosawa's Dreams*

Malick, Terrence
1998 *The Thin Red Line*
2005 *The New World*
2011 *The Tree of Life*

Marker, Chris
1962 *La jetée*
1977 *A Grin Without a Cat*
1983 *Sans soleil (Sunless)*
1985 *AK*
2006 *Chats perchés (The Case of the Grinning Cat)*

Ozu Yasujiro
1934 *Ukigusa monogatari (A Story of Floating Weeds)*
1936 *Hitori musuko (The Only Son)*
1941 *Todake no kyodai (Brothers and Sisters of the Toda Family)*
1949 *Banshun (Late Spring)*
1951 *Bakushu (Early Summer)*
1952 *Ochazuke no aji (The Flavor of Green Tea over Rice)*
1953 *Tokyo monogatari (Tokyo Story)*
1956 *Soshun (Early Spring)*
1958 *Higanbana (Equinox Flower)*
1959 *Ukigusa (Floating Weeds)*
1960 *Akibiyori (Late Autumn)*
1961 *Kohayagawa-ke no aki (The End of Summer)*
1962 *Sanma no aju (An Autumn Afternoon)*

Pasolini, Pier Paolo
1964 *Il vangelo secondo Matteo (The Gospel According to Matthew)*
1975 *Salò*

Renoir, Jean
1937 *La Grande illusion (The Grand Illusion)*

1939 La Règle du jeu (The Rules of the Game)
1951 Le Fleuve (The River)

Rossellini, Roberto
1945 Roma, città aperta (Rome, Open City)
1950 Francesco, giullare di Dio (Flowers of St Francis)

Tarkovsky, Andrei
1975 Zerkalo (Mirror)
1979 Stalker
1982 Tempo di viaggio (Voyage in Time)
1986 Offret (The Sacrifice)

Truffaut, François
1959 Les Quatre cents coups (The 400 Blows)

Welles, Orson
1958 Touch of Evil

Wenders, Wim
1973 Alice in den Städten (Alice in the Cities)
1975 Falsche Bewegung (Wrong Move)
1976 Im Lauf der Zeit (Kings of the Road)
1977 Der Americkanische Freund (The American Friend)
1982 Chambre 666 (Room 666)
1982 Stand der Dinge (The State of Things)
1984 Paris, Texas
1985 Tokyo-Ga
1987 Der Himmel über Berlin (Wings of Desire)
1991 Until the End of the World
1993 In weiter Ferne, so nah! (Faraway, So Close)
1994 Lisbon Story
1996 Die Gebrüder Skladanowsky (A Trick of The Light)
1997 The End of Violence
2000 The Million Dollar Hotel
2003 The Soul of A Man
2004 Land of Plenty
2005 Don't Come Knocking
2007 Invisible Crimes
2007 War in Peace
2008 Palermo Shooting
2011 Pina

Acknowledgements

We are grateful to Carolin von Roth, Heidi Frankl and Stefanie Röders for their assistance and their tremendous help in the various stages of the manuscript production.

Many thanks to Leonard Cohen for *The Land of Plenty* lyrics. Sebastião Salgado for permission to use his photograph in our book. Thanks to Spanish branch of Doctors Without Borders for permission to use *Invisible Crimes*.

We would like to thank the School of Social Sciences, University of New South Wales, for help with funding the short films for the website design and display.

We would especially like to thank Jerry Sohn for his hospitality and generosity in letting us stay at his cabins near Joshua Tree while completing the manuscript. We give special thanks and gratitude to Donata Wenders for her insights, love and grace. To Liza Thompson for her inspiration and to Keith Jacobs for his help and to Jane Butler, Sylvie Sweatmen and Peter Sweatmen for their love and support. And thanks to Mary's father, the late Spiros Zournazis, who taught her the necessity of patience, hope and peace.